Advanced
Rockcraft

Advanced Rockcraft

by

Royal Robbins

illustrated by

Sheridan Anderson

Cover photo by Steve Essig

LA SIESTA PRESS
1973

related La Siesta publications:

Ruth Dyar Mendenhall
BACKPACK TECHNIQUES

Royal Robbins
BASIC ROCKCRAFT

Walt Wheelock
ROPES, KNOTS & SLINGS FOR CLIMBERS

LA SIESTA PRESS
BOX 406
GLENDALE, CALIFORNIA   91209

ISBN 910856-56-7

Contents

INTRODUCTION 7

CHOCKCRAFT 9

BIG WALLS 55

GADGETS 62

SAFETY 65

LEADING 67

SOLO 71

VALUES 78

FANTASIA (a story) 85

INDEX 95

Introduction

In general, what humans want from an instruction book is to become good at something without spending the time to learn it totally on their own. Very likely they don't have that much time. And, unless one is making a game of ignorance, it is only intelligent to want to know as much as you can about something you are doing. So we fork out a few dollars, spend some time reading and practicing, and expect this investment of time and money to pay dividends. It is not an unreasonable expectation, but I must warn the reader not to expect much from this book. I offer no easy solutions, no real shortcuts. The burden of this book is that climbing, even fun-in-the-sun rockclimbing, involves anguish. I have yet to meet a climber who does not occasionally experience it: the expert faced with a difficult and poorly protected lead, the intermediate contemplating a route one grade harder than any he has managed before, the boulderer about to try a 20-foot route which will require all the skill and strength he possesses, any of a hundred leaders halfway up a pitch frozen into immobility by fear of continuing and reluctance to give it best.

This book will stress that you get out of climbing exactly what you put into it, that the only kind of climbing that is ultimately worthwhile demands a spiritual effort that is sometimes agonizing. That safety is almost totally a function of character and common sense, that the only way to climb properly and safely is to exercise painful self-restraint and discipline, and to realize that just getting up a route is nothing, the way it is done is everything.

For a number of reasons I have been tardy following up *Basic Rockcraft* with this sequel. It is just as well, for climbing has changed rapidly in the interim, and I would not have written this book the same way two years ago. One big change is in the dramatic increase in the number of climbers. This has influenced the sport in many ways, but perhaps most importantly it has focused attention upon the necessity of employing methods of climbing which are non-destructive. This has meant a general change to use of artificial chockstones instead of pitons, which by their removal and replacement erode the rock. In 1967 I wrote an article for *Summit Magazine* extolling the virtues of artificial chockstones, but failed to convince many. I had little luck promoting chocks in *Basic Rockcraft*. But in the last two years the pace of conversion has quickened, helped considerably by Doug Robinson's article on "Clean Climbing" in Chouinard's catalog and by the efforts of John Stannard. Chocking has become fashionable.

In fact, the increase in numbers has only accelerated the transformation from pitons to chocks which would have occurred anyway. Attention is being focused upon the destructive aspect of pitons with special urgency because of

the numbers of climbers using them. But the change to chocks would have come anyway, as part of an evolution toward a finer game.

Modern rockclimbing calls for a new consciousness, a new rock ethic (new to the U.S., at least). Instruction books, guide books, climbing schools and clubs, and established voices in the climbing community have no higher duty than to foster the attitudes and uses of rock which will preserve routes as we would preserve works of art — for future climbers to enjoy in as nearly as possible their original state.

Climbing is a great game — great not in spite of the demands it makes, but because of them. Great because it will not let us give half of ourselves — it demands all of us. It demands our best.

Chockcraft

The essence of *chockcraft* is art. With pitons one can attack many a pitch with little fear, little art, little skill, yet with impunity. For when the going gets rough, whack-whack-whack- in goes the pin, we clip to it, and bulldoze our way upwards. If we restrict the use of pitons, and instead employ chocks or natural runners, we are playing a different and deeper game. We play it just as safely, but not in the same way. For example, we cannot attack a pitch with the careless aggressiveness that characterizes our approach to a 2″ jam crack knowing we can sink a bong at will. We must give more forethought before committing ourselves, for we can't necessarily sink nuts wherever we wish. Formerly in American rockclimbing speed has seemed important. This was partly due to the length of the routes in many parts of the country, but partly too, it was due to the concept that if you had good protection, why fiddle around? Go ahead and boulder it and if you fall, try again. Thus by placing reliance in the piton we could increase our confidence and zip up. Pitons formed a barrier between us and the rock. In those comparatively rare times when we couldn't get protection from pins, we were forced to become more intimate with the rock, to work more on its terms — *to climb better.*

Mistakes happen. Hence the use of the rope and pitons and chocks for protection. But chocks will in most cases be enough if we will just see those parts of ourselves for which pitons are the substitute.

Chocks preserve routes, and help us minimize the impact each of us has upon the rock. But they offer other rewards as well. What a pleasure to climb a fine route and find no traces of those who have come before and to leave no mark of one's passage. What a pleasure to climb the quiet way — without hammering — to use art instead of force. What a pleasure to take one's time and work out the placements not obvious — to put one's creative energies to work fashioning a lead that is both safe and silent.

Wired chocks
photo by Royal Robbins

[9]

Slinging trees, spikes, natural chockstones, small tunnels and such features is making use of natural runners. For this purpose, webbing is more useful than rope. Sewn slings made of flexible, flat webbing are lighter, trimmer, and easier to use than slings formed with knots. And if properly stitched they are stronger as well. Longer slings (which double as runners over large blocks and as diaper seats) are best carried doubled over the head with a carabiner to equalize the lengths.

CHOCKSTONES A chockstone is a rock wedged in a crack. It is stuck because the crack narrows downward. If the crack narrows sharply, or slowly but continuously, the chockstone is well-wedged, i.e., as long as the force is downward, the stone cannot be pulled out without disintegrating. A poorly-

wedged chockstone is one in a crack that narrows only slightly, and even worse (but not unusual) one which after narrowing opens again. A slight crumbling of the edges of either the chockstone or the surrounding rock will allow the stone to drop. If the stone is not solid, consider moving it elsewhere in the crack where it will wedge better.

TREES AND BUSHES are obvious objects for natural runners. Beware of small one which are shallowly rooted. For rappelling, place a separate sling around them, for repeated retrieval of a rappel rope from around a small tree will damage it.

TUNNELS AND ARCHES in solid rock provide one of the most secure of natural runners as they are solid from pulls in any direction. A length of medium stiff wire is useful for threading such holes, as well as for threading natural chockstones.

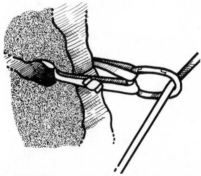

HORNS, FLAKES, SPIKES, BOSSES, AND CHICKENHEADS provide another valuable type of natural runner. In some areas, such as the Needles of South Dakota, such protrusions form a critical part of the protection system. Some horns are obvious, some are not. It is essential to be constantly alert for them. Even a questionable horn is better than none

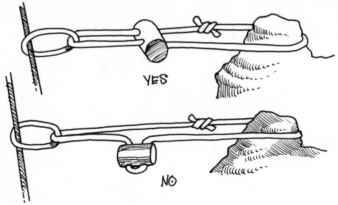

for the runner *may* stay on. Sometimes a rope, or more likely, webbing, can be slipped behind a flake that is barely detached from the rock.

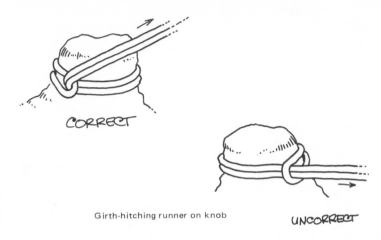

Girth-hitching runner on knob

KEEPING THE RUNNERS ON

Once your alert eyes have spied a horn it is important to use it to best advantage. If the horn is prominant and the notch deep there will be no problem unless the rope angles sharply above the horn. In this case the runner can be secured with a girth hitch, or by weighting with extra gear, or by anchoring it to a fixed point below. Such a fixed point might be a chock slotted upward or a sling around a downward-jutting horn.

If the horn is rounded, and the notch shallow, it will be harder to keep the runner in place. Webbing is better than rope for this use, as it will contact a larger surface area and have less tendency to roll off. Flexible flat webbing is preferred over tubular as it has less tendency to creep. And of course, narrower webbing will have an advantage over wide on small horns. To keep runners on poor horns the above methods may be used; however, by definition a poor horn cannot be girth-hitched. Generally, the best solution is to attach a runner which will allow the sling to lie more quietly on the knob. This also lessens the chance of lower runners being pulled off when the rope goes taut in a fall. When using runners on knobs, try to arrange them so a fall will not cause them to be flicked off (see illustration, page 30). And don't use just one poor knob when several poor ones are available.

BE AWARE

One must cultivate skill in searching for security in natural features. There are more natural runners than you think. But you must be alert for them. Don't carelessly reject those on easy ground, there may not be one higher.

Charles Pratt on Salathé Route, El Capitan
photo by Tom Frost

ARTIFICIAL CHOCKSTONES (NUTS)

Artificial chockstones operate in the same manner as natural ones. We carry a variety of shapes and sizes and select the one which forms a good wedge. Generally this means using the largest chock the crack will take. Three basic shapes are round, hexagonal, and wedge. Most are designed to fit at least two sizes of cracks.

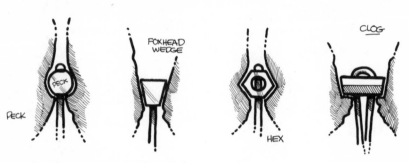

WIRED CHOCKS AND SLUNG CHOCKS

Besides being stronger, cables have the advantage of allowing one to place the chock five or six inches beyond one's reach. In addition, the short cables are helpful in aid climbing where one is using the chocks to gain height. The disadvantage of wire is that the chock can be more easily dislodged by rope drag if the rope runs at an oblique angle. This isn't usually a problem in aid climbing, as the chocks are normally closer together and the line straighter.

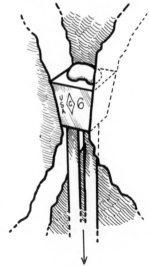

But in free climbing the stiffness of the wire and the ease with which it can lever the chock is a serious consideration. To some extent, the single cabled chocks have an advantage here, for they are more flexible and therefore exert less leverage. The double-cabled chocks are helpful in awkward placements which require precise movements of the chock deep in a crack. The double cable also helps in removal as one can usually pop the nut by pushing on the cable, especially if the wire is epoxied to the top of the nut.

For free climbing, chocks on nylon rope or webbing are preferred. These can be slung on runners made from material four to five feet long and easily carried around the neck.

ROPE OR WEBBING?

In deciding to thread chocks on webbing or kernmantle rope, there are considerations of strength, esthetics, and utility. In esthetics, rope wins, for most chocks have circular holes which more logically accept circular section rope, whereas they distort webbing. But in terms of utility, webbing is better because it will slip into a thinner crack below the chock than will rope. Webbing and rope are about even in strength. Tests by John Armitage, Tom Frost, and John Stannard indicate little difference between the strongest webbing and the strongest rope one can get through the holes in a given chock. Rope, however, is superior in terms of *wear,* for webbing, having a larger surface area, will abrade more easily and lose its strength more quickly. Both webbing and rope should be replaced when they show substantial signs of wear. If there is any doubt, the decision ought to be on the side of prudence.

Some find the greater utility of webbing decisive and much prefer it to rope for chocks, but one can have the advantages of both by mixing the selection.

SLINGING CHOCKS

Use the largest webbing or rope which will fit through the holes *without difficulty*. If the fit is too tight, it will be hard to adjust the sling on the nut. Often it is desirable to do so.

For chocks carried around the neck use material about 4½ feet long. Chocks on short slings can be carried on the hardware loop like wired chocks or pitons. Carried so, they are less bothersome, but unfortunately are less useful. Most free-climbing placements require a full length runner to allow the nut to sit quietly as the rope moves upward, and for aid climbing cabled

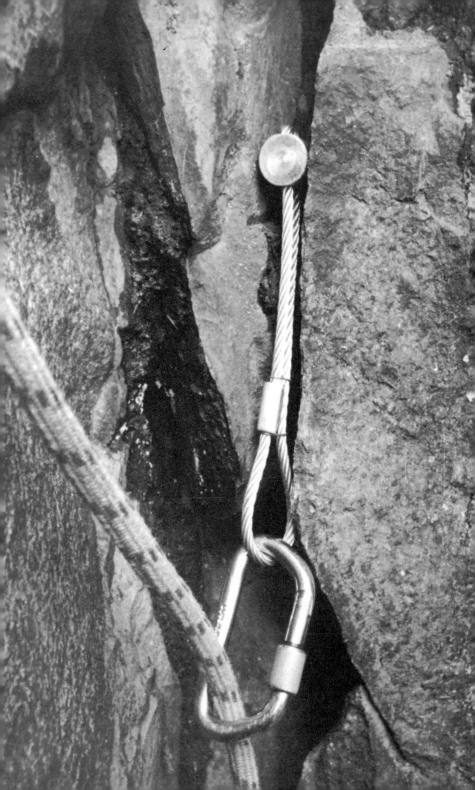

chocks have obvious advantages over short slings. One can extend the short sling with a runner, but this is an extra operation, and one must often contend with the bulkiness of the knot precluding a good fit of the nut. An exception is with large chocks. These don't come wired, so they will be most versatile if carried on short slings (see illustration for a convenient way to carry large nuts).

KNOTS

The ring bend (water knot) is satisfactory for forming runners and threading chocks. It is easily tied, strong, neat, and requires a minimum of rope. Tie it so the ends protude about two inches and then bounce on the sling so the knot is solid and tight. The ring bend (as any knot) should be checked occasionally to assure it remains properly tied.

There are stronger knots one might use, but such knots are rarely useful because, unless the rope is *unnecessarily thin,* the weak point of the sling will be at the *chock.* It will be at the chock unless one is using sub-standard size rope, such at 7mm in a 9mm hole, but why do that? Likewise, if one is using 7mm for a general purpose runner (no chock involved) the strength of the knot may be significant because it would probably be the weak point. But the proper size for such purpose is 9mm. which isn't going to break anyway (unless it has a weakened spot, and that's not likely to be in the knot). In short, there is little justification for the greater bulk, weight, and expense involved in knots stronger than the ring bend.

COLOR CODING

Reserving a color or style or thickness of rope or webbing for each style and size chock is a great help in selecting the nut you want when hanging by one hand and searching with the other. It is also useful to have all normal runners (slings) of one color, and double-length slings of a color or size different from the rest.

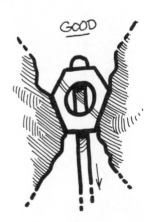

GOOD

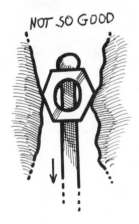

NOT SO GOOD

CHOCKING

For a chock to work, it must form a good wedge, which simply means there must be sufficient taper in the crack below the chock to prevent it being ripped out. But the taper won't help unless the rock is solid. Decomposed rock or soft rock must be watched carefully, as must cracks lined with lichen or moss which will make the crack appear narrower than it is.

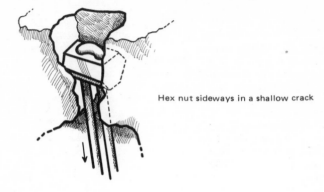

Hex nut sideways in a shallow crack

Example of crack requiring large nut but thin sling (webbing)

Any slot formed by irregularities in the rock may do.

If the chock is well-wedged and the rock is solid, the weakest link will normally be the sling or wire. It takes enormous force to break heavy chock cable or one-inch webbing or 9mm rope, but in the smaller sizes some concern over the strength of the material attaching the carabiner to the chocks is reasonable. One must operate largely on common sense in this area because we can't accurately gauge the force generated in a fall. And common sense dictates prudence. It appears, however, that it takes a pretty long fall to generate forces in excess of 2,000 pounds. In fact, the stretch in modern ropes, plus the natural resiliency of the belayer and the "give" built into the mechanics of the belay itself make it unlikely that a force of 2,000 lbs will be achieved in a fall. The stretch in an 11mm rope which conforms to the

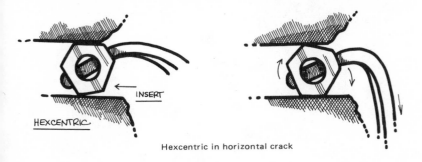

Hexcentric in horizontal crack

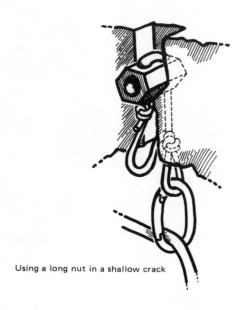

Using a long nut in a shallow crack

UIAA (Union International des Associations d'Alpinisme) standards will allow a force of about 2,500 pounds at most, (simulating the worst possible fall), and this in a carefully rigged, totally artificial situation next to impossible to achieve in the field. So although we would not want to be overly sanguine about links of the belay chain holding in a fall, it is comforting to know that those links which test to 3,000 pounds are probably secure in *any* fall.

But whether your protection will hold 1,000 pounds or 5,000 pounds, it is unwise to trust your life to it. Trusting one point of protection if there is a real chance of falling is something I would do only in extraordinary cases. Get on as many runners as possible, so if one breaks (absorbing some of the force in parting) the others are there to back it up. It is quite possible that a fall generating forces up to 2,000 pounds (as unlikely as that is) might be stopped by three nuts carrying 5mm rope because the top ones, in parting, would absorb some of the force. Even nuts carrying 4mm line or thin wire can stop short falls, or sliding ones, or in breaking absorb part of the force of a longer one.

PROBLEM

With our chock well-wedged in solid rock, and a reasonable expectation that the sling is strong enough to hold a fall, all is well as long as the chock stays in place. Here we come to one of the critical elements of the art of chocking. The problem is simply that chocks which are solid when pulled downward may be lifted from their mooring with an upward force. There are several ways this can happen and several ways to prevent it:

BODY — The body is away from the rock as you move past the chock, causing an upward and outward pull on it. And often the knee catches the rope below the chock, lifting the rope and the chock as well. *ROPE DRAG*— If the chocks walk a crooked mile, with the rope running diagonally from one to another, the rope, as it runs diagonally upward may dislodge them.

A nut on a short sling may be pulled out by the body as the climber moves past

[21]

Beginning the Direct Route on Half Dome
photo Liz Robbins

FALLS — Similar to the rope drag problem, but more serious. A hard fall on a rope running back and forth between nuts could lift all but the top chock, and if that chock then failed, the results, with all back-up points eliminated, I leave to the reader's imagination.

SOLUTIONS

Try to place the chocks in a straight line. Seat them with a sharp downward tug (in extreme cases tapping lightly with a hammer may be called for, but this must be regarded as driving a piton. I formerly held the position that a tapped nut counted as a piton only if the rock showed the effects. Unfortunately this delicate criterion is too often mis-used and badly smashed, permanently driven nuts are the result). Be careful when moving past the chock, and especially watch the knee. It may help to place a hand or foot over the top of the sling to hold the nut in place. Another solution is to anchor the chock against an upward pull by attaching the sling to a chock slotted upward, or a sling around a downward pointing horn, or anything else which can be anchored against an upward pull.

An easily overlooked possibility is slotting a nut in a horizontal crack to prevent rope drag from dislodging a vertically anchored nut (see illustration, page 34).

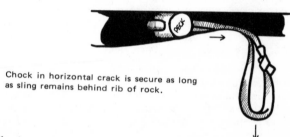

Chock in horizontal crack is secure as long as sling remains behind rib of rock.

But generally the best solution, whether to avoid the body pulling the chock out or rope drag or a fall doing it, is to extend the sling on the chock by using a runner, or in extreme cases, several of them. This lengthens the

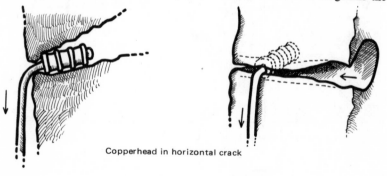

Copperhead in horizontal crack

distance one will fall, but greatly increases the chance of the chock remaining in place. Guard against the built-in reluctance to do this because of a slightly longer fall, it's better than having the chock pull out. If there is any doubt about whether a runner is needed on a chock, put it on. To quote John Stannard, "It is a rare nut that requires less than a full length runner." *Note —* Some of my British friends are adamant in insisting that the answer is double rope technique as commonly practiced in Europe. In general, this adds an unnecessary complication, but there are times, especially on traverses, when it could be useful.

CHOCKS IN HORIZONTAL CRACKS

Although chocks are more naturally suited to vertical cracks, horizontal placements are often secure. Two main opportunities present themselves: slots, and opposite-pressure wedges. For slotting, all that is needed is an opening big enough to accept the chock, and which, on one side or the other, partially closes on the surface but remains large enough inside to allow the nut to be slipped sideways. Such slots are common beneath arches and flakes. Wired nuts are superior for this use because they are easier to maneuver.

If the crack slots sideways but does not close on the surface, it can still be used if the sling can be passed over a ridge, hump, or edge of rock.

OPPOSITION

If the above doesn't work, perhaps opposition will. This is slotting two (or more) chocks in opposite directions in a horizontal crack and linking them so any force pulls them toward each other, wedging them more securely. This idea was discovered while experimenting with chocks at one of our *Rockcraft* climbing courses, and first publicized in an advertisement in *Summit Magazine* for "Peck Crackers." Climbers were at first loath to accept it, but it has now become a commonly used means of obtaining security in horizontal cracks. It must, of course, be used with discretion, because it is often difficult to judge just what the force of a fall will do to one's protection system.

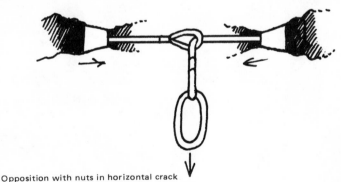

Opposition with nuts in horizontal crack

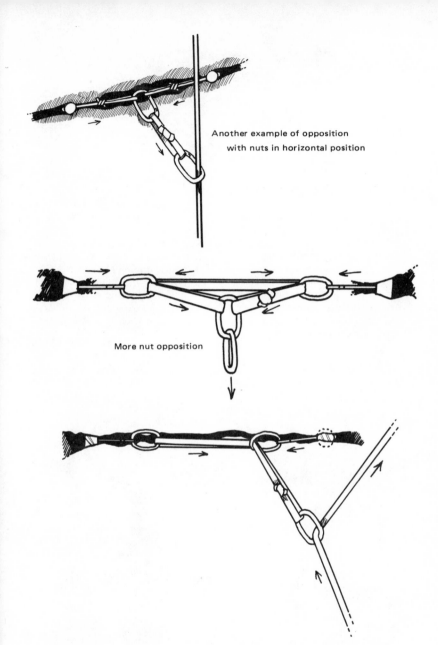

Another example of opposition
with nuts in horizontal position

More nut opposition

Nut on left is less secure. A long sling assures a horizontal pull on it, while allowing a more outward pull on right nut, which can resist the outward force.

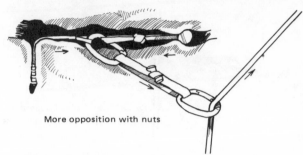

More opposition with nuts

The chocks should be clipped together as tightly as possible. Probably the best placement is when two chocks can barely be connected with a carabiner, for a fall will pull the carabiner straight, wedging the chocks even more securely. Other possibilities are illustrated. If the chocks are far apart, one can be extended with a long sling, and this run through a carabiner attached to a short sling on the other (preferably the more secure one). This will cause a horizontal pull on the long slinge chock and a minimum outward force on the short one. A safety sling on the short runner nut might be in order in case the long sling nut pops and pulls through the carabiner.

Sometimes, even when a single chock in a horizontal crack is adequate to hold a falls, an opposition chock will be used to keep rope drag from pulling the security chock out.

VARIATIONS

Bongs with holes at the tip can be used as chocks. Many other things can substitute for regular chocks, such as carabiners or knots. The security these

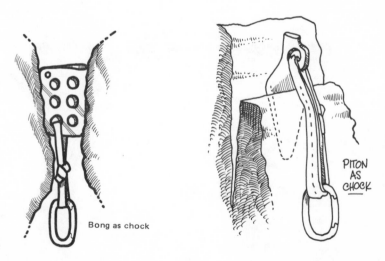

Bong as chock

PITON
AS
CHOCK

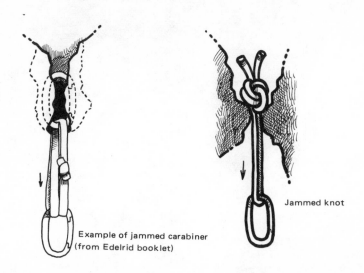

Example of jammed carabiner
(from Edelrid booklet)

Jammed knot

give will at times be dubious, but they are better than no security at all. A piton placed in a normal position without pounding qualifies as a chock. This can rarely be done in a vertical crack, but it is an ever present possibility in horizontal cracks, straight down behind flakes, and in holes.

ANCHORS AND BELAYS

In placing chocks for a belay anchor the same methods apply as for leading, but one must pay even more attention to assuring the soundness of the system — it is the court of last resort. It is important to be especially alert to the possible directions of force in a fall, particularly, but not so obviously, a pull upward. The various suggestions given above, such as chocks slotted upward, are relevant here.

The *location* of the belayer is also important. Difficulty arises most commonly when the belayer is not directly below the climber. If he is away from the rock or to the side, the rope will form an angle which will tend to be eliminated by an upward pull if a fall occurs. An obvious solution is to belay directly below the climber, but this is not always possible or even advisable, for the belayer is then robbed of the benefits of friction in holding a fall, and subject to danger from rockfall. Another solution is to find a belay point resistant to an upward pull.

CARRYING ENOUGH

Because one tends to place more chocks than pitons and because there is normally less choice as to which chock to use in a given placement (e.g., you can force a ¾" angle into a ⅓" crack, but not a ¾" nut), and since it wise to get as much security as possible, it is extremely important to carry a good supply of nuts, with a wide range of sizes, and plenty of carabiners and runners to extend the nuts. It is a common error to underestimate how many chocks, carabiners, and runners one will need, and it is much better to have

[27]

too much rather than too little. One might easily place 15 chocks on a sustained pitch, along with 10 runners for extensions or horns, and 25 carabiners. When one is moving up a long difficult pitch in unknown territory, 25 chocks, 30 carabiners, eight regular runners and two double runners is not excessive.

If you are going to use nuts, use plenty of them. If you can get two for protection at one spot, use them. You might be wrong about how good one is. The other will back up your judgement.

REUSING THE SAME NUT

It is sometimes possible to reach down and remove a chock below for replacement above. A variation of this technique is to attach a long runner or series of them to the top of the sling in the nut and retrieve it when you reach a place where the nut can be re-inserted. This technique is especially suited for wider jam cracks because one is more likely to need to reuse the same nut as an alternative to carrying many large heavy ones.

REMOVING CHOCKS

In placing chocks, security is the primary aim, but the leader should also think about taking them out. Sometimes it is necessary to place the nuts so removal is difficult, but only rarely.

A sharp upward pull will remove most chocks and possibly the glass in your spectacles. Often, wedge-shaped chocks will not succumb to this approach, and must be gently lifted with the fingers. A long thin piton helps reach those the fingers can't, and a light hammer to tap the piton upward against well-wedged chocks is a useful tool. An occasionally handy technique is pulling the sling through the nut and lifting it out by pulling straight upward on the sling.

Chocks with a loop of cable instead of a single wire can usually be dislodged by pushing upward on the cable. If the cable slides too easily through the nut, it can be secured with a bit of epoxy glue.

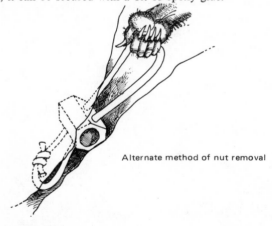

Alternate method of nut removal

Use of a normal machine nut

Before attempting to remove the chock, determine which method of removal is best. Otherwise you may wedge it further. The most frustrating are those which have been placed in an opening and have dropped down into an enclosed area behind. It is tempting to give up, but it should come out. It is usually a matter of finding the key.

LEARNING CHOCKCRAFT

Two methods are helpful in learning the art of chocking. One is to do easy climbs and to place nuts and runners wherever possible, whether needed or not. The other is to practice aid climbing with nuts. These methods will sharpen one's awareness of the nutting possibilities that exist, and improve one's ability to judge the stability of a given placement.

LEADING WITH CHOCKS

Leading with chocks is more than finding good slots. A typical lead with chocks and natural runners demands many things be brought together to form a whole, and that whole is an artful and safe lead of the pitch, using as much as possible the natural features, and placing and connecting protection in such a way that it works together without contradictions within the system. In constructing a system of protection, one must always be thinking of the impact of a fall on the *entire system*. Thus it may be unwise to sling a doubtful bush if the rope going taut in a fall will pull one's lower runners off just as the bush is breaking. And unless the rope runs in a straight line between climber and belayer, there will in a fall, be a sideways and upwards pull on all points not in a straight line. If possible there should be nuts slotted upwards or sideways to protect the stability of nuts off the straight line.

But rather than rules or techniques, leading with chocks is a matter of exercising maximum awareness of the rock, of our own limitations, of the power and directions of forces in a fall, and of our equipment and its weaknesses and strengths. One must be nearly as possible one with the rock, so one's actions do not contradict the rock's potential. The "climb" becomes not merely making the hard moves and reaching the top, but the entire experience, with the creation of a logical system of protection as much a part of the ascent as the actual climbing.

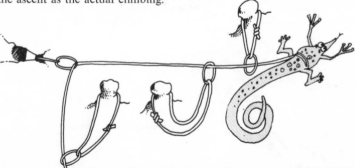

A protection system. Horizontal nut prevents pull of rope from removing runners. Runners are long enough to allow rope to run straight.

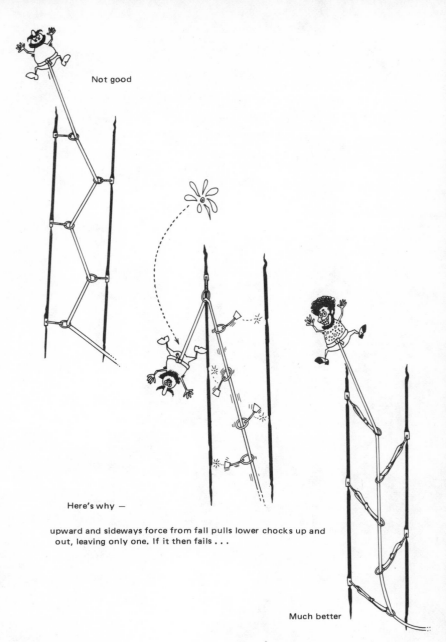

Not good

Here's why —

upward and sideways force from fall pulls lower chocks up and out, leaving only one. If it then fails . . .

Much better

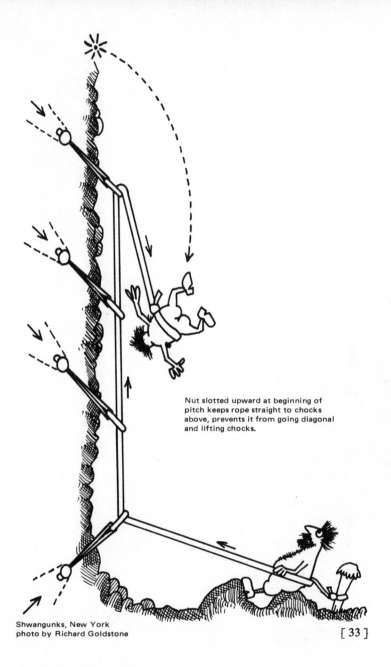

Nut slotted upward at beginning of pitch keeps rope straight to chocks above, prevents it from going diagonal and lifting chocks.

Shwangunks, New York
photo by Richard Goldstone

Horizontal nut, useless for holding fall, keeps rope drag from removing vertical nut, which may hold a fall.

Aid

In the previous volume we discussed the fundamentals of piton and nut placement, and the mechanics of following an aid pitch. We here talk about leading and more sophisticated placements as well as a few new bits of equipment.

Anything goes in aid climbing, anything, that is, except using a bolt that is not necessary. It is absurd to place bolts freely on an aid route, for the very point of the aid game is ingenuity and craft in using whatever natural features the rock offers. Bolts can be used anywhere, so their careless use contradicts the reason we are on the rock. Better get an extension ladder or walk around the back side. Bolts occasionally make possible a fine route otherwise impossible, and therein lies their sometime justification.

The aid game, properly played, can be fascinating, for it can demand all of one's ingenuity and discipline. But aid climbs that are much used become caricatures of themselves. It becomes a game of getting pitons to stick in man-made holes — artificial climbing even more artificial. Using nuts will reduce this problem, and all-chock ascents of aid routes can become an admirable and exciting game in itself.

Even if one doesn't like aid, it must be learned in order to do big walls. Some of the greatest rockclimbs in the world have substantial sections of aid.

LEADING AID

This is a matter of getting some sort of gadget to stick to the rock and using it for progress. Although pulling on a carabiner attached to a piton, stepping on a piton, or resting on one, are all considered aid, normally aid involves the use of *etriers* (in the Alps, aid climbing has long been defined *as* "the use of etriers").

PLACEMENTS

Place and test pitons or nuts as described in *Basic Rockcraft*. All aid pins need not be driven as well as those used for belay anchors or free climbing protection. When in doubt, one should drive a piton as well as possible, but a sense of proportion is useful. In an easy aid crack, each piton should be placed well enough to do its job — that is, well enough to hold a fall resulting from misjudgement about how well you will drive the next peg. As experience is gained it is possible to cut the line finer and place pins closer to the margin, but we are here entering a realm bristling with traps for the unwary. Very experienced climbers cannot always tell when a piton is good, even in an easy crack. Beware the prejudice against overdriving pitons — it is a narrow and foolish viewpoint. Nowhere has this hare-brained prejudice gotten a firmer grip than Yosemite Valley, where several 100 foot falls have occurred as a direct result of social pressure against overdriving steel. It shows just the sort of romantically twisted thinking that causes 99% of all rockclimbing accidents. So, if you err, err on the side of overdriving, and show the proper sign to your partner if he bitches.

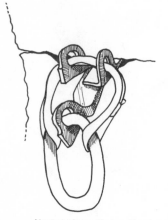

Nested pitons tie together to prevent loss

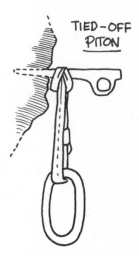

TIED-OFF PITON

HARD NAILING

Hard nailing is a matter of getting something to stick to the rock either through pressure or wedging or a combination of the two. Pressure is obtained through driving a piton into a crack — the pressure against the sides keeps the piton in place. Wedging is discussed thoroughly in the chapter on chockcraft, but with pitons the wedging should occur through the crack narrowing both above and below the piton to prevent pivoting. Of course, the object driven can be any variation of a piton, and we need not have a crack — any configuration of the rock that will support a wedged or driven object will do.

When the nailing gets thin, one must keep sight of the two principles of wedging and pressure. At the same time keep the mind open to the most unorthodox and imaginative possibilities in using these principles, separately or together. And we can add a third principle to the above — that of *minimum leverage*. This is obtained by, for example, using short pitons in shallow

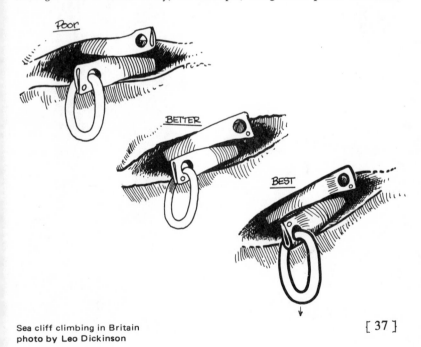

cracks, or by tieing off the piton next to the rock. Leverage can also be minimized by clipping to a hole nearer the tip of a bong, or by placing a knot or nut in the crack and driving the the piton just below so the weight comes onto the tip of the pin. Stacking or nesting pitons is a common way of filling a shallow crack. Again, the aim is to get enough sideways pressure to keep things in place. One advantage of stacked pitons over a short wide one is that two or more pitons together provide a certain resilience, a sort of spring action against the sides of the crack. Stacked pins are usually tied off close to the rock. Attach a safety sling through the eyes of the pitons to save them if they come out.

Piton pinning copperhead against back of crack for minimum leverage in shallow crack

NAILING LOOSE FLAKES

The problem with loose flakes is that as you drive succeeding pitons, those below are loosened by prying action of those being placed. This can be minimized by using chocks whenever possible, using long pitons with minimum taper, and not driving them too hard. It is often useful to clip to the piton you are driving with a spare sling in case the one holding you pops.

CAMMING

In an article in *Summit,* March 1972, Greg Lowe introduced the concept of using cable loop and piton combinations to climb even-sided cracks without hammering. The piton and cable are inserted into the crack with the cable on the side of the piton and the piton is wedged tight by a sharp downward tug on the cable, giving a wedging or camming effect. Additional weight on the wire wedges the piton more firmly. The principal advantage of this technique

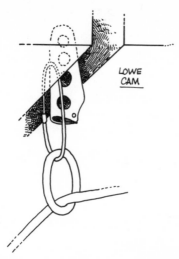

is avoiding damage to cracks where chocks cannot be used. However, they may also confer a benefit when nailing expanding flakes because they won't expand the flake as will a driven piton. Camming appears to be most useful in softer rock, where the piton and cable can bite well. It would be wise to thoroughly experiment with this technique before extending oneself. Rope will work in place of wire, but it gets cut up pretty fast.

RURPS

These were described in *Basic Rockcraft*. One of their great virtues is they can punch their way into seams that are not really cracks. This gives them great holding power, for they are in effect wedged in a hole from which it is difficult to lever them. What leverage exists is minimized by the carabiner attachment being close to the rock.

BLOBIES, SMASHIES. BASHIES,

and other malleable pitons, are of soft metal — usually aluminum — that conform to the rock and harden upon impact. They are especially suitable for use in rounded, shallow grooves, where RURPs are useless. More and more they are used in holes created by what were once RURP cracks being enlarged by repeated hammering of larger and larger pegs. Used in this way bashies become one more step in the degradation of routes, for they can rarely be removed and become difficult to use after the sling breaks. Driving a horizontal piton along the sides is usually the answer. Bashies with wire sling might be another.

COPPERHEADS

Bill Forrest's gift to the aid climber, these are copper swages on wire. Their greatest utility is in very shallow cracks or grooves. Like the bashies, they are soft enough to conform to the rock, but they have the additional

advantage of the wire coming straight from the bottom of the swage, eliminating leverage. Copperheads also function quite well as nuts and can make use of the shallowest slots.

SKYHOOKS

These are useful tools for aid climbing. The best design was invented by Jim Logan. The Logan hook has the advantages of keeping the pull close to the rock, and of being non-pivoting due to legs which stabilize either side of the base.

LOGAN HOOK

ROPE THROWING

When one is faced with an area that can't be nailed, chocked, sky hooked, or freeclimbed, the classical method of lassoing a horn is suitable and in the finest tradition. On the south face of Watkins a blank section is passed by throwing a rope over a small tree. And once while attempting to solo a new route on El Capitan, I saved six bolts by hurling artificial chockstones into cracks. This technique is most useful for crossing short blank sections, and must always, of course, be used with discretion.

MOVING UP

After you have driven the piton or placed the nut, use etriers to advance. You will find it is extremely easy to get totally wrapped up in your work. When learning, don't rush. Take your time and work out the pattern of movements. They are as follows: clip the rope to the carabiner at the placement, clip in the etrier, climb up in the etrier as high as balance will permit and stand with one foot in aider and one in sub-aider (or in second etrier), make next placement and repeat. An alternative method is to clip in the etrier first and climb up and clip the rope in when one is waist high to the piton. Ideally, the second system is more efficient, but in practical use each variation has its advantages. For example, a disadvantage of the second system (advocated by

RURPS and Bashies

Chouinard) is, if there is considerable rope drag and the next piton is poor, moving onto it and dragging the rope too will increase the force on it, not something you wish to do. Another is, if the pin pops and the rope is not clipped to it, one may lose the piton and all the gear attached. Either variation of the Yosemite Method is adequate in straightforward nailing, and any dogmatic approach is confounded when the nailing gets awkward or difficult.

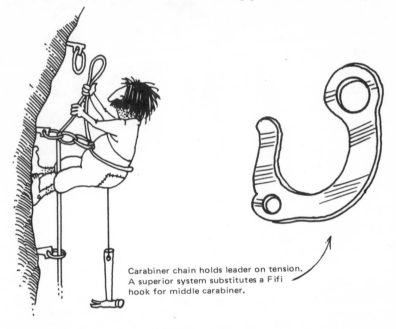

Carabiner chain holds leader on tension. A superior system substitutes a Fifi hook for middle carabiner.

If the angle is not steep, one should be able to stand in the top loops. This is desirable as it will minimize the number of placements. As the wall steepens we are forced lower in our etriers, but still strive to make the placements as far apart as possible. It helps if the belayer holds the rope taut. Sometimes this doesn't work because the rope stretches. A simple solution is to clip a fifi hook on a carabiner attached to one's waist loop to the piton. On steep or overhanging rock this fifi hook technique offers the further advantage that one can take in the rope and clip it to the next piton while still being comfortably held on tension.

CLIMBING OVERHANGS

Here it is especially useful to clip the rope to the next placement before advancing. Keep yourself from falling over backward when pulling up the slack rope by bracing in the rest position or by using a fifi hook as described above. After clipping in, use the self-pulley method to advance (i.e., pulling downward on the climbing rope after it has gone from one's waist through a carabiner at the placement).

In aid climbing, as in free, keep the body away from the rock. When you must use your arms, move up quickly and rhythmically and get into the rest position or on tension and get the weight off the arms. When using the arms to move up, keep them straight. This will enable the bones instead of the biceps to do the holding, and will keep the body further away from the rock, allowing easier raising of the legs.

Self pulley

FRICTION

One must be constantly alert to guard against getting too much friction in the system. This is done primarily by extending our carabiners with runners, but it may also be occasionally useful to unclip from problem placements to allow the rope to run more reely. Such unclipping must, of course, be done judiciously so one does not incur the risk of a long fall. Remember to minimize the friction low on a pitch, before it becomes a problem; otherwise it may become intolerable later.

PRACTICE

There are numerous mistakes in rope and etrier management which everyone makes when learning aid climbing. Much practice is necessary to acquire smoothness and efficiency in progressing with rope and etriers.

CLEANING

The mechanics of following and piton removal are described in *Basic Rockcraft*. One should add to these the importance of getting into the best position for removing the piton. This will generally be the rest position, with the piton waist-high or a bit lower and the body away from the rock so one can swing the hammer with force and accuracy.

JUMARS

Using Jumar mechanical ascenders to second an aid pitch is faster and easier than seconding in the classical fashion. For big wall climbing, or even for short routes that are totally aid, the efficiency of the Jumars more than compensates for their additional weight. There are other mechanical ascenders on the market, some as good or better than Jumars for straight ascents of ropes. But for following aid routes Jumars are incomparably better.

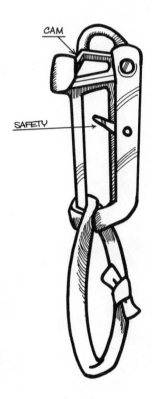

First day, El Capitan
photo Tom Frost

USING JUMARS

First, attach slings to the bottom of the Jumars. I prefer two web slings of 5/8" or 9/16" width on each Jumar, but a single sling of 1" should be satisfactory. These slings will abrade on the corners of the Jumar, so one must inspect them often.

A formula for how long slings should be and where one should attach them for prusiking is hard to come by. With the use of etriers with sub-aiders (see *Basic Rockcraft,* pages 15 and 31), this problem is nearly eliminated as the aiders are already "set up" for Jumaring. If you do not use etriers with sub-aiders modify the following instructions according to your equipment: 1) Attach two carabiners to waist loop. 2.) Attach right Jumar to rope. 3.) Clip aider to Jumar and top loop of sub-aider to right carabiner on waist loop. 4.) Attach left Jumar to rope below first, clip second aider to it, and clip lower loop of sub-aider to left carabiner on waist loop. 5.) Put right foot in third loop of right aider and left foot in second loop of left aider. 6.) Slide the top Jumar up as far as possible and stand in sling attached to it. Weight should come about equally on your right leg and waist. 7.) Slide second Jumar up to first. 8.) Transfer weight to second Jumar, and, straightening lower leg, stand up in one smooth motion, sliding the top Jumar upward as far as possible. A bit of practice will enable one to do this with minimum effort. When you slide the Jumar upward, unweight the foot, except for a light touch which keeps it in the etrier.

SEPARATE POINTS

1.) At first, the lower Jumar will lift the rope when you try to slide it up. To avoid this, release the cam each time with the thumb until you are high enough for the weight of the rope to make this unnecessary. 2.) The sub-aider sling which attaches to the waist loop should be in good condition. Replace when it becomes frayed. 3.) Always be sure that *both* Jumars are attached to your body. 4.) The angle of the pitch will determine how much weight comes upon the waist, how much on the right foot, and how awkward in general is the ascent. The perfect angle for Jumaring is about 80 degrees. If the angle is very low, keeping the body vertical becomes difficult because the waist attachment to the top Jumar is too short. Lengthen it by attaching to the *second* loop of the sub-aider instead of the first. When the angle gets even lower, it is best to remove the feet from the aiders and walk up, a Jumar in each hand. If, on the other hand, the ascent is very steep, and especially if the feet do not touch the rock, a diaper seat sling attached to the top loop in the top etrier will make the trip much more comfortable. A chest harness also helps. 5.) Left and right may, of course, be reversed. The right Jumar is the one which, when held in the right hand, has the thumb on the side of the cam and safety catch. 6.) Most of the points above apply equally to prusik knots or other types of ascenders.

SECONDING WITH JUMARS

Ascend as described to the first placement. Remove the climbing rope from the carabiner at the placement and clean the piton or nut. Usually, it

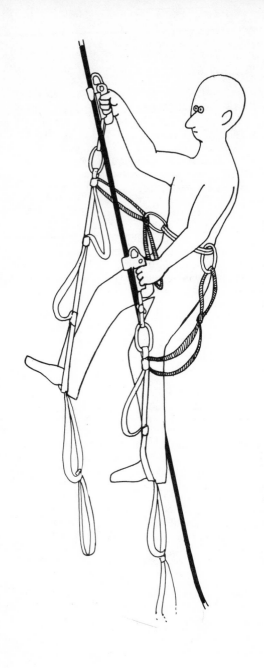

is necessary to remove the top Jumar from the rope and reclip it above the nut or piton, before one can unclip the rope from the carabiner. Continue in this fashion. If the placements are in a fairly straight line, and if the pitch doesn't overhang, the foregoing pattern should present no problems. For greater security tie to the end of the rope. In Yosemite this has resulted in at least one climber's life being saved, and another might have lived had he been attached. If the seconding is at all problematical, as on traverses or overhangs, tie off just behind the Jumars with a figure-8 loop to minimize a fall if the Jumars fail. Another useful safeguard is to tie a prusik knot between the two Jumars and attach it to the bottom Jumar. Then, if the bottom Jumar fails while the top is off the rope, one may still live.

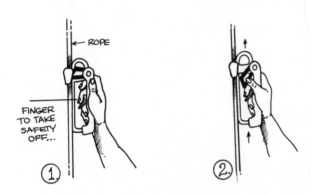

Method of removing Jumar from rope

TRAVERSES, SHARP DIAGONALS, AND OVERHANGS

These present problems, the principal one being that when the top Jumar is placed above the piton it cannot be weighted without jamming the second Jumar against the piton. The solution is to use the same method as for following pendulums (see below). The only difference is that one normally does not need to untie from the end of the rope to pull it through, but can reach back and unclip it.

PENDULUMS AND TENSION TRAVERSES

These are methods of moving horizontally across a blank section of rock. A pendulum involves swinging on the rope and a tension traverse is working across with friction of hands and shoes while being held on the rope. Pendulums can be easy or they may prove the most difficult part of a climb, depending upon the arc and upon the holds one is going for.

When leading, it is simply a matter of the second lowering the leader far enough for him to swing or claw his way across the blank area. In some cases

this will involve being lowered only a few feet. In others it may be a hundred or more. After making the pendulum the leader should climb as high as he safely can before clipping in the climbing rope. This will make the second's job easier.

There are several methods of following a pendulum, and they normally involve leaving some gear, such as a piton and carabiner, at the pendulum point. The most straightforward method with Jumars is as follows: 1.) Remove the top Jumar and replace it on the rope above the pendulum point. 2.) Grasp the rope below the second Jumar and remove all weight from it, being supported by the first Jumar and by gripping the rope below the second Jumar. Slowly pay out the rope by moving the second Jumar downward in stages, using it for support when necessary. 3.) When across the traverse, transfer the second Jumar to the rope below the first, untie from the end of the rope and pull it through the carabiner at the pendulum point and tie in again.

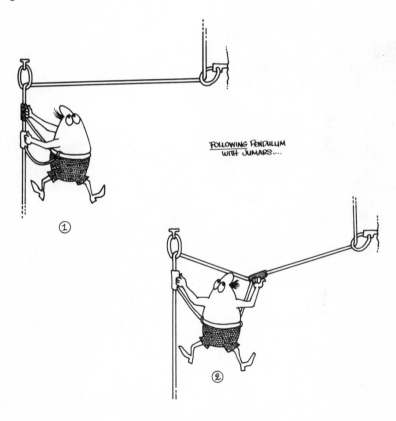

FOLLOWING PENDULUM
WITH JUMARS....

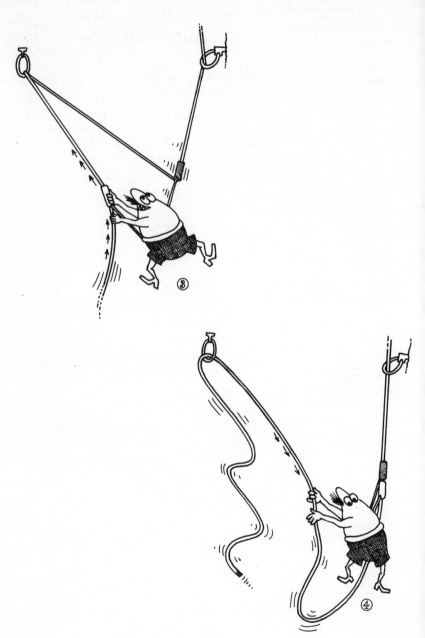

The above method works best on short pendulums where the rope runs horizontally or diagonally upward. But if the traverse bridges a large gap, or if the rope runs downward from the pendulum point, the following method is recommended. 1.) Same as above. But if the rope runs downward from the pendulum point, proper placement of the Jumar will cause it to be inverted, the bottom toward the pendulum point and the top toward the ground. 2.) Fashion a carabiner brake and run the rope below the second Jumar through it. 3.) Remove the second Jumar and attach it next to the first. 4.) Rappel until it is possible to Jumar to complete the traverse. 5.) Untie to retrieve rope.

It is possible to follow a pendulum without sacrificing a carabiner by using a doubled second rope and rappelling.

If the second is not using Jumars, it is easiest for the leader to lower him from a carabiner at the pendulum point until he can swing and complete the traverse as the leader did.

It is essential that the pendulum point be reliable, otherwise the second may take a long fall. If there is any doubt, two or more anchors should be left. And there should be doubt nearly always. Also, never allow a rope to run across another rope under tension.

SAFETY WITH JUMARS

While there are other ascenders which can be used in climbing, Jumars have the edge in efficiency. They will, however, slip on icy or muddy ropes. Gibbs ascenders are recommended for such conditions.

Although very efficient, Jumars must be used with respect. Misuse of them has caused death and injury. A death occurred in Yosemite when a climber neglected to attach the Jumars to his waist. He went all the way because he also wasn't tied to the end of the rope. This may seem obvious, but one of the top big wall climbers in the country learned his craft by following the entire Leaning Tower (an 1,100 foot overhanging wall) without being clipped to his Jumars. It is easy to overlook the obvious, especially when one's attention is absorbed by the challenge of a great wall.

There is an insidious danger that is peculiar to Jumars. This is the chance that they may be placed on the rope without the safety trigger in locked position. This can happen easily on a diagonal rope. One must be certain that the rope is in the slot, that the cam is biting against it, and that the safety trigger is in the locked position. This is usually quite easy to assure when used on a rope running vertically, but a mistake can be made when the rope runs diagonally. If the Jumar is clipped to a diagonal rope with the shaft held vertically, the cam may prevent the safety trigger swinging into place. To avoid this the shaft should run parallel to the rope when attaching the Jumar. Check visually to assure the Jumar is properly attached. The back-up of a prusik is advised.

DEVICES

Various devices, such as seat and chest harnesses, adjustable etriers, decenders, etc., have their use in limited situations, that is, short or specialized aid problems. If, for example, you have a 300' route which overhangs its en-

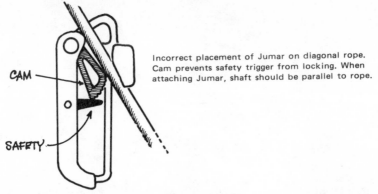

Incorrect placement of Jumar on diagonal rope. Cam prevents safety trigger from locking. When attaching Jumar, shaft should be parallel to rope.

tire length and has a 30-foot ceiling in its middle, paraphernalia especially designed for such situations will be useful. But the Yosemite approach to aid technique is based on big wall climbing, which demands spare methods suited to a variety of climbing problems, rather than specialized techniques which work well on one part of the climb, but get in the way on other sections. Specialized gadgets and techniques will tend to reduce the overall efficiency. For this reason, Yosemite climbers have always tended toward the starkest simplicity in aid techniques — it works better on big walls.

If, however, you find other approaches, other techniques, other types of equipment work, by all means, use them. Manufactures of alternative equipment will generally furnish information on use. This book will discuss some in a separate chapter.

Big Walls

In rockclimbing, a big wall loosely refers to any climb of say, 1,000 feet or more. But a stricter definition, and one that suits our purposes, is any Grade V or VI, normally requiring a bivouac, and involving substantial amounts of aid climbing and big wall techniques. The great faces of Yosemite, the Diamond and Black Canyon in Colorado, Mt. Hooker in the Wind Rivers, and the Squamish Chief in British Columbia are examples of big walls.

Many are the joys and challenges of free climbing on small crags, but a big wall adds another dimension. It demands a greater variety of skills and qualities, and a deeper commitment. On a big wall one is isolated, and this isolation is a source both of apprehension and satisfaction, often more of one than the other, depending upon how much one feels in control.

How to climb a big wall? I can't tell you. But the sensible way to learn is to first climb little ones. Then you can make your inevitable mistakes in man-

Big Wall east of upper Yosemite Fall

agable surroundings and acquire the experience necessary to cope with difficulties in a more severe environment. In short, there is no substitute for experience, but the following points may crystallize what you are learning.

TECHNIQUE

It is necessary on long climbs to move smoothly and competently, and to minimize mistakes. For the actual climbing, the techniques described elsewhere in this book are used, the difference being that on a big wall these techniques are used in a sustained way. And since the distances are large, efficiency in rope work, hauling, etc., is essential. One need not be a speed freak to take pleasure from moving up a wall smoothly, but one area often overlooked is what the man who is not climbing can do to help. He often sits on a ledge as if stunned, or in a sort of reverie while belaying or waiting for the second to clean, when he could be sorting hardware or untangling rope, or doing other bits and pieces to help along the enterprise.

Leading is usually done with an 11 mm rope, and a 9 mm line for hauling and rappeling. Ropes 150 feet long are sufficient for most routes, though very occasionally a 165 foot rope is useful.

When the route includes traverses, a 7 mm rope is often a useful supplement to the 9 mm hauling line. It effectively lengthens the hauling line, so that if one is more than 100 feet out on a traverse, he can still easily fetch gear from the belayer without the necessity of the belayer letting go the end of the hauling line.

YOSEMITE METHOD

The Yosemite method of climbing big walls incorporates a less strenuous way of hauling with a technique of following a pitch (Jumaring) which does not require a belay. Not only is Jumaring a faster way to follow an aid pitch, it also frees the leader from the task of protecting the second man so the leader can do the hauling.

It works thusly: the leader leads, and anchors the rope at the top of the pitch. After freeing the haul bag so the first man can raise it, the second cleans the pitch by Jumaring up the fixed rope. Hauling is done by arranging a pulley system so the weight of the body and the force of the leg can be applied. The line to the pack passes through a carabiner (or even better, a simply pully), and a Jumar is attached to the free end. An etrier is attached to this Jumar and a foot goes into the etrier and pushes down. *Voila* — the sack rises. The sack is prevented from slipping back by suspending the other Jumar upside down on the haul line on the back side of the pulley. A sling of hardware can be used to keep the reversed Jumar steady.

HANGING BELAYS

These are common on big walls. Unless one is using bolts, three anchors should be a minimum for a hanging belay. When *belaying* the second man, anchor to the two lower points and belay through the middle and upper ones. The middle anchor will safeguard the other two. If the second man is *Jumaring,* fix his rope to the top anchor, and also to the middle. The leader hangs from the lowest anchor and is anchored to it as well as to the middle one, and

hauls from the *middle* one. **These combinations spread the** stresses, and provide back-up in case one part of the system fails. Other combinations are possible, but the principles should be the same. A belay seat helps.

GEAR

Equipment required will vary according to the temperatures and the weather of the region and the season. Prepare for the worst, not the average or the likely, but the worst possible. Bivouac gear will normally include wool shirts, sweaters, gloves, extra wool socks, a *duvet* (down jacket), and waterproof *cagoule*. A duvet is worthless if it gets wet, so every effort must be made to keep it dry. It might be wise to pack your duvet in a waterproof bag during a wet storm, rather than wear it. It will then be dry when the rain stops and the temperature drops, and that is when you will need it. For wet conditions, wool is the best natural insulator. Much body heat can be lost through the head, so a good wool hat is advised. The best ones are the Scottish *balaclavas* which can be adjusted to cover the face and neck in storm. A foam pad can provide excellent insulation and also is the best way to pad the hauling bag. The rope can be used to fill dips in the ledge. Two-man bivouac sacks conserve heat, and are especially protective in a storm. Finally, heat tabs or a light stove are a pleasant luxury that allow a cheering brew on a cold morning.

FOOD

This depends upon one's taste, but should be selected with the mountain environment in mind. Anything that doesn't readily rot should never be jettisoned, so it is best to avoid canned goods, as the environmental conscience will demand carrying the empty cans to the top. Nuts, salami, and the right candies are easy to carry and involve minimal packaging.

WATER

Experience on less serious climbs will teach you how much water you need. Depending upon the weather and your thirst, it may very from less than a pint per day to more than two quarts. In any case, it must be carried in tough plastic bottles with strong lids.

FIRST AID

It is wise to carry a first aid kit including a wire splint or plastic inflatable splint, and to know how to use everything in the kit.

MISCELLANEOUS

Often useful are: sun glasses, sun cream, hat with visor, light headlamp, and salt tablets.

HAUL BAG

This should be constructed of durable material, strongly stitched, be large and roomy, have hauling straps that are especially strong, and double as a pack for approaching and descending from the climb. It must be carefully packed so there are no sharp corners, and be well padded, preferably with a foam pad. No pack, however tough, if it is poorly packed or poorly padded, will long withstand the rigors of hauling over rock. A separate day pack, which

Camp 5, 2,300 feet, El Capitan
photo Tom Frost

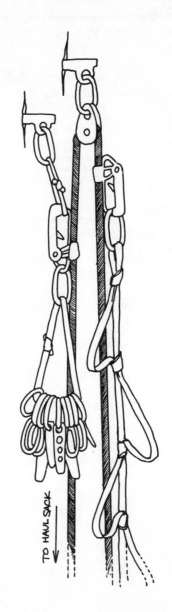

TO HAUL SACK

Method of hauling

can be either hauled or carried by the second, can be used for sweaters, water, sun glasses, or other items you wish easily available.

BIVOUACS

Although not all big walls require bivouacs, a night out is a distinguishing characteristic of the genre. I remember my first one vividly. It was on the Pedestal on Yosemite Point Buttress. Jerry Galwas and I were making the second ascent. We huddled, shivering most of the night, we didn't mind the discomfort, because we didn't know any better. Now, with duvets and foam pads one can pass a night on a wall in comfort, almost in luxury, though what one gains in comfort is lost in intensity. These days, bivouacs, assuming fair weather, are not to be avoided, but rather to be relished. It is a pleasure to pass a night on a wall because of that very feeling of isolation mentioned earlier. One is in limbo, cut off from the crowd, suspended between mighty efforts of the day past and the day to come. There is a feeling of satisfaction. All that matters is the ledge, the companion, nuts, cheese, and salami, having enough water, the anchor that makes one as solid as the rock, and the great starry night.

There is an art to bivouaking, but you will soon enough learn by doing. It's basically quite easy. You stop on a ledge, secure yourselves and your gear, eat, drink, put on warm clothes, and pass out. If you can't pass out because of too little or too much fatigue, or because you aren't used to a firm bed, no matter, you pass the night watching Orion or the Great Bear tick the minutes off the celestial clock, until that faint greying in the east that you have been awaiting turns to light blue, and then so slowly to yellow. If you are watching at the right moment the sun will appear as a bubble of molten gold boiling up between two peaks. It lasts only a moment, but it's worth waiting for, and you won't have a choice anyway.

HANGING BIVOUACS

With hammocks, hanging bivouacs are not necessarily less comfortable than ledges, but they are much more trouble because there is no place to set the gear. Everything must be hung or kept in the haul sack, and handled with the greatest care.

If possible, the hammock should be strung from points at least six feet apart. A single point suspension can be rigged by shortening the straps on one end.

Gadgets

Although I personally prefer climbing methods that are spare, there are climbers (and the number is growing) who see advantages in equipment not strictly necessary. They may be right, at least for themselves and the type of climbing they do. Here are several items which may interest the climber for various reasons:

SAFETY HELMETS

In England, hard hats are worn by most climbers, including the best, and they are used by many safety conscious climbers in North America. They do reduce the risk of head injury, but it has never been established whether the man wearing a safety helmet is more or less likely to have an accident than the man without one. It would be consistent with human nature that wearing a helmet would make one more likely to venture into dangerous situations. It would make one more likely, for example, to climb behind another party on a route with loose rock and therefore to incur the risk of receiving a rock too big for any helmet. If, however, one is exposed to rockfall and can't do anything about it, wearing a helmet will reduce the chance of head injury. The problem with helmets is they are a bother. The individual must decide for himself whether the greater safety the helmet might offer in his climbing is worth the bother. There are two things involved here, one is the feeling of security that helmets might give, and the other is the actual security. If it is a feeling of security one is after, little more can be said. One is clearly in the market for a hard hat. The question of true security is much more difficult. One has to make as shrewd an appraisal as possible about the chances of getting hit with a rock. Natural rockfall is rare in pure rockclimbing areas, and if one can avoid climbing behind other parties, and always climbs with a partner who is alert and cautious, one is very unlikely to get hit by a rock. On the other hand hard hats also might help protect the head in a tumbling fall. Some climbers seem to have an instinct for protecting their head while falling, while others don't. Here again it is a question for individual evaluation and decision. One thing seems clear, though, and that is that the decision about helmet use should be a rational choice, not one based upon fashion or mystique.

SEAT AND CHEST HARNESSES

In Europe harness rigs of one sort or another are common, so there must be a lot of climbers who are finding them useful, or think they are. The utility of harnesses lies in the following: they decrease the risk of injury from the rope in a fall (the risk, however, is slight, as witness the thousands of leader falls sustained on simple tie-in without injury), they reduce the risk of suffocation from hanging on the rope after a fall (this has killed climbers, but the percentage is minute compared to the number who have fallen), they allow one to do free prusiks or overhanging aid with less strain. The trouble with harnesses is that they are a bother and are superfluous most of the time. A simple harness can be arranged by fashioning a diaper seat. However, if one desires a more elaborate rig, a combination seat and chest harness seems a logical answer.

DESCENDERS

These are specialized rappelling devices which do the job well, but involve carrying an extra piece of gear. They have the advantage over carabiner brake rappels that they are simpler and hence less prone to accident. The figure-8 design seems to be the most fool-proof.

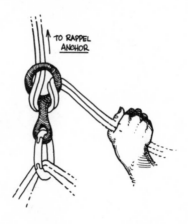

Figure 8 descender

STICHT BELAY PLATE

A simple device to help a belayer hold a fall, or sustain the leader on tension. It works by cinching. A bight of the climbing rope is placed through the slot in the plate and clipped to a locking carabiner. If a fall occurs, the belayer moves the free end of the rope sideways, forcing the plate against the carabiner, snugging the rope. The disadvantages are that the belayer cannot manage the rope as quickly and easily, and the rope does not pass around the body. If the system fails, the belayer is left with the rope only in his hands, and that makes an ineffective belay. This is a more complicated way to belay, and involves carrying an extra piece of equipment.

The plate does, however, make it possible for a light person to hold a heavy one in a fall involving little friction. The number of Sticht plates sold in the United States is increasing rapidly, evidence that many climbers are finding them useful. The plates come with various combinations of notches for belaying with different sized ropes, or double-rope technique. They also make satisfactory rappel devices.

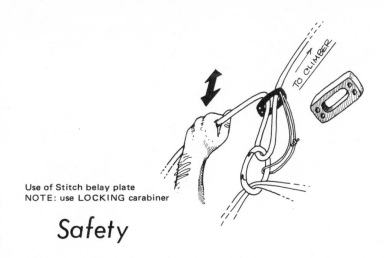

Use of Stitch belay plate
NOTE: use LOCKING carabiner

Safety

Danger is always present in rockclimbing (in the final analysis it is an essential ingredient), but it can be kept in control by an exercise of prudence and will. But one must realize where danger lies.

MOUNTAIN HAZARDS

Storms, lightning, and natural rockfall, are sometimes problems on alpine rock climbs or big walls. They are more properly a subject for texts on mountaineering, and the reader is referred to Blackshaw's *Mountaineering* and *Freedom of the Hills* for advice. There is also an excellent article on "Lightning Hazards to Mountaineers," by Alvin E. Peterson in the 1962 *American Alpine Journal.* But the best thing to do about lightning is to stay off high places when cumulus clouds are building.

ROCKCLIMBING DANGERS

Unlike mountaineering, most rockclimbing is free of objective dangers. One real one, however, occurs when climbing behind another party, which may dislodge loose rock, drop equipment, or fall on those below. These dangers can be avoided by not climbing behind other parties. A more insidious problem occurs at the base of popular cliffs where climbers traversing the slopes above can dislodge loose rock. One may be well advised to wear a hard hat in such areas.

But the principal danger to the rockclimber is falling off the rock himself, rather than rock falling upon him. This danger presents itself in two ways — through failure of judgement and through failure of equipment.

FAILURE OF EQUIPMENT

Accidents resulting from failure of equipment can be avoided by not putting all one's trust in a single link of the safety chain. Use, for example,

Cerro Torre, Patagonia
photo by Royal Robbins

two slings for a rappel instead of one. And, don't risk a fall onto a single nut, no matter how solid, if a failure of that nut or the carabiner or the sling means disaster. Modern equipment is so strong that failure is unlikely, but faulty gear is nevertheless a real possibility, even when it comes from reputable manufacturers. By using two or more items to do the same job we can reduce the chance of total failure to insignificance.

FAILURE OF JUDGEMENT

This is the primary cause of rockclimbing accidents. "Judgement," in this sense includes self-control, common sense, and mental alertness, as well as the exercise of prudence, and of clearly seeing the reality of a climbing situation, and the reality of one's capacity to respond to it.

An example of failure of judgement occured to me at Tahquitz Rock after I had been climbing three years. As I was nearing the end of a long lie-back, I got careless and tried to rush it, grabbing in my haste a loose rock. A 25-foot fall resulted. My piton held, and I was not seriously hurt, but it was a foolish thing to have done. This fall was not "due to" loose rock, and if the pin had pulled, a further fall would not have been due to a piton "failure." Although it is true that I would not have been so careless had my piton not been good, still, because it took me totally by surprise, the fall was due to my failure as a climber, to a laziness of the mind and will. And had the peg pulled, that would have been due to bad judgement in placing it, not to its "failing."

Safety in rockclimbing lies almost entirely within this "judgement" area. Little is left to chance. Equipment is a minor factor. With the best equipment in the world, the man with poor judgement is in mortal danger, whereas he who has sound judgement is safe with nothing but tennis shoes because he will not venture beyond the limits of his equipment and capabilities.

If we are keenly alert and aware of the rock and what we are doing on it, if we are honest with ourselves about our capabilities and weaknesses, if we avoid committing ourselves beyond what we know is safe, then we will climb safely. For climbing is an exercise in reality. He who sees it clearly is on safe ground, regardless of his experience or skill. But he who sees reality as he would like it to be, may have his illusions rudely stripped from his eyes when the ground comes up fast.

We are, of course, all mixtures of sanity and folly, of clear vision and murky romanticism. Such conflicts are a mark of the human condition. And we climb because we are human. The rock is a field of battle between our weakness and our strength. We wouldn't touch rock if we were perfectly self-controlled. And he who would climb and live must continuously wage this battle and never let folly win. It's an outrageously demanding proposition. But I never said it was easy.

Leading

Why lead? The mystique of *first on the rope* has a romantic aura, but little necessary relation to the joy of climbing rock, whether leading or following. When climbing with a competent leader who provides a secure rope from above, there is little risk, and one can savor the pleasure. And on a good route one can find a lot of excitement without going first. But someone must go first, and there are those who love the special demands made only upon the man on the sharp end.

LEARNING TO LEAD

In learning any new craft it is important to practice in a familiar environment. Otherwise the distractions of too many new elements, and fear of the unknown, will slow learning. A sound approach is to start on routes which one has followed, and which are well within one's ability, and progress to harder routes as judgement and ability to place protection increase. In this way skills and confidence are gained with less risk of getting into those desperate positions so common to inexperienced leaders.

SELECTING A ROUTE

Before attempting a climb you have not done, be sure it is well within your capabilities. To this end, consult guidebooks and the opinions of persons who have done the route. These will generally give a reasonably accurate grading. On the other hand, regard route gradings with some skepticism. Grading systems are notoriously inexact languages. Although useful, they must be used with care. The grade of a climb is nothing more than the consensus of those who have done it as to how difficult they found it. The fact that a route is graded 5.7 is no guarantee that you will not find it harder than other routes of the same grade. One may find it much harder for a number of reasons, among them: being unfit, being off form, that the route is on strange rock, that unfamiliar techniques are required, that the route has been altered, that one is off route, or that the judgement of those forming the consensus was warped. So when using grading systems, expect the worst and hope for the best. When in doubt it is usually better to heed your personal evaluation. If you do not see your way clearly as to how you are going to do something, don't trust the guidebook, your friends, the competitive urge, or logical constructions telling you why you *should* be able to do it. To hell with all that. Trust your instincts.

ROUTE FINDING

The challenge of route finding is to first climb with the mind, and then to have this mental ascent tested against reality by finding out if the body can go where the mind did.

In selecting a line two considerations must be weighed. One is ease of climbing and the other is availability of security. Although these usually follow the same path, they don't necessarily, and it may be desirable to accept

more difficult climbing if the protection is better. Thus one may choose a difficult crack offering good slots for chocks, over an easier face studded with holds where a fall will end all.

Generally, it is better to follow cracks as they often provide security as well as holds. When the crack lies in a corner, it is even better, as the walls of the corner usually offer scope for bridging and other pushing techniques.

On steep walls or difficult climbs it is important to rest occasionally to recover strength. So select your line to include resting places, but realize the view from below can be distorted. What appears to be a good ledge often is a nasty sloping shelf. Or the wall above may be so steep that the ledge is useless for resting. Even the most crafty cragsman can climb into trouble by misjudging a stance from below. So be careful that wishful thinking does not warp your judgement.

CLIMBING

After one has chosen a climb and ascended it mentally, the action begins. Before starting, assure that everything is in order. Check the position and anchor of the belayer, the knots in one's rope and harness, the selection of chocks and runners, their ease of availability, the knots in slings, and whether one has everything one needs, such as the hauling line. Use the techniques described in *Basic Rockcraft,* but remember that the importance of many points is magnified because the penalities for error are greater. The comments about loose rock, for example, are especially pertinent. Every hold is suspect.

Important to the leader are husbanding his strength and staying out of trouble. He can save strength by minimizing effort, by staying off his arms except when necessary, by using good technique, and by resting whenever possible.

He stays out of trouble by climbing in stages, never leaving a stance until he knows exactly where he is going, what he will do when he gets there, what he will do if he doesn't get there, and what he will do if, getting there, he finds not what he expected. To some extent, the leader can use reserves of strength to escape from difficulties once he has mistakenly climbed into them. But he must always be keenly aware of how much strength he has left. He must anticipate the drain upon his physical resources by being alert to the ebbing of strength in his forearms and fingers, and by climbing down before it is too late.

PROTECTION

The leader places protection to support his judgement. If he blunders, he then will not pay the ultimate penalty. At least so he hopes. But the security is rarely fail-safe, so the leader should not be too surprised if it pulls and he takes a longer fall than he hoped. Further, if the leader relies upon his protection to save him from the consequences of his mistakes, he may be more likely to make them. He would be better advised to stay within his ability, and never put the protection to the test. On the other hand, it is reasonable for an expert to take a serious risk of a leader fall by attempting something at the limit of his ability if his protection is ample and the landing free of hazards. This sort of pushing, however, is not a normal part of the art of leading.

In any case, the protection must be placed in such a way that it does its job. Protection placed carelessly may be worse than none at all if it gives a false sense of security. The alert leader will also anticipate the need of protection and place a runner too soon rather than too late. Better to drop in a chock early, than wish you had one when no slot is available.

And as we pointed out in the chapter on Chockcraft, whenever the leader is far from his protection, he must move slowly. He must substitute time for runners.

If the leader, having fallen, cannot be lowered to a ledge or climb back up the wall, he will be unhappy. He will be even sadder if he is hanging from his waist loop. Such situations are rare, but must be anticipated by rigging a seat harness for the problem pitch (or wearing one constantly), and by carrying rope slings and runners so he can prusik out of trouble.

ROPE DRAG This is one of the most exasperating problems with which the leader must cope. Here, as in placing protection early and in avoiding cul-de-sacs, one needs to look ahead. Anticipate the problems by avoiding bends in the rope low on the pitch. Carelessly placed runners may create rope drag which, though minor at first, may become intolerable later.

RESPONSIBILITIES OF THE LEADER

Besides the necessity of climbing within his ability and the limits of his protection, the leader faces many obligations concerning the welfare of his partners. If, for example, the leader choses a climb too difficult for the second, and the second has a miserable time, the fault is entirely that of the leader. But there are more important considerations. The leader must guard against a long fall not only for his own sake, but in consideration of his partner. He owes the second the kindness of placing as many runners as possible to lessen the seriousness of any fall. Even on easy ground he should whenever possible get *something* between himself and his belayer, if only for the peace of mind of the belayer.

And the leader must find solid anchors before bringing up his partner. It is disagreeable to climb a long and difficult pitch to find the leader belaying from a manky nut or piton.

TRAVERSES Traverses present another area demanding maximum awareness at the sharp end. It is part of the leader's job to always arrange good protection for the second. Problems sometimes arise when a difficult move is followed by an easy traverse. The inattentive leader may place good protection before the hard move, but neglect to place some just after. This leaves the second facing a long fall if he slips from the rock on the difficulty.

SELF-CONTROL

The essence of being on the sharp end and doing it well is maintaining the finest of razor edges between desire and fear — the desire to get up and fear of the rocks below. Leading creats an inner tension which must be maintained by those who would climb safely. This tension can be dissipated by the sensible course of retreat, or by the foolish course of blind and desperate effort. But whoever would get up difficult ground through design and not chance, that is to say competently, must be willing to fight a continual inner battle.

So don't expect leading to be anything but demanding. It is a severe discipline, and although free use of pitons, bolts, and chocks can take the edge off, they cannot entirely eliminate the seriousness. And there come those occasions when equipment is useless. The competent leader must develop self-control as a form of self-protection. He judges the best he can. He sizes things up. It looks like a good crack. He goes for it, across a long difficult traverse and finds the crack worthless. Now he has climbed into trouble, he must get out. Rigorous self-control will be his best means of escape.

But by self-control I don't mean only that kind needed to escape from a hazardous situation. That is important, but not so much so as the self-control needed to avoid getting into a pickle in the first place. Judgement and instinct tell one where it is safe to go, but still it takes self-control to keep the romantic impulse from over-riding good judgement or displacing it. It takes self-control to accept the limitations of one's abilities, whether they be due to lack of experience, of strength, of technique, or to simply being unfit. Such self-control is never easy. It is acquired by vigorous battles against the temptation to yield to weakness. It is worth the effort to achieve.

Some may argue that this chapter makes leading appear unduly severe, that it often is not like that, that on the contrary, when one's blood is coursing, when the day is beautiful and the rock is fine, when the route is delightful and one's companions are comrades, then indeed the crags ring with the shouts of pleasure expressing the exuberance of climbers, whether leading or following. True. But there come those inevitable days when one will find everything I have said in this chapter to be true, and though the memories of anguish and anxiety tend to fade quickly with time ("It was a piece of cake," he said, two hours after a fearful grip-up.), they were non-the-less real and distressing when they occured. The leader doesn't need to be prepared for the best, but rather for the worst. He doesn't need to be prepared for what rockclimbing is most of the time: good fun.

Solo

I am pulled in different directions writing this chapter. On the one hand I don't wish to encourage solo climbing. The mountains are more dangerous when one is alone. Probably the greatest danger of solo climbing is its addictive influence. It's a strong shot, and one hungers for more, tending to draw the line finer, and when that happens a possibility exists of the appearance of a morbid note, and then the joy vanishes.

On the other hand, for those temperamentally suited to it, soloing has its rewards as well as its terrors. I have been often asked about the techniques involved, so I know there is a demand for the knowledge. And I feel a further

obligation to provide information for those who at times must solo, as when one's partner has been injured.

There are two basic types of solo rockclimbing — roped and free. In roped soloing one protects oneself by belaying. Free soloing is climbing without a rope or other protection.

ROPED SOLOING: There are two main approaches to solo belay systems — full pitch and staccato. The full pitch system involves climbing an entire pitch, then descending and retrieving one's gear. The staccato method is suited to climbs on which one needs to protect oneself only over short sections.

STACCATO: The principle here is moving the protection along in a sort of stop-and-go pattern. Many methods exist.

One method uses only a short length of rope, say up to 50 feet, and attaches that rope as necessary to protection points, usually tying in with figure-8 loops at any point along the rope where it is convenient. When one is past the short section of difficulty, anchors placed above will allow one to descend to remove those below. Several points should be stressed: 1. Always keep a figure-8 attached to you. 2. Horns and chocks will often provide protection which allows the rope to be retrieved by simply pulling upward. 3. If your anchor below is secure against a pull upward, don't tie the rope to subsequent belay points, but rather just pass the rope through the carabiner. This will allow a more dynamic belay. In fact, the more rope you have out relative to the distance of a fall the more gently will that fall be held. The worst fall you can take is one twice the distance of the rope used in holding it. It is worth remembering that a mere 20 foot fall held by 10 feet of rope tied off to a static anchor is more severe in terms of the forces achieved than a 200 foot fall on 150 feet of rope. 4. Don't fall. Solo belay systems, even more than normal belay systems, should be viewed as a last resort method of staying alive. They are not to be trusted to hold a fall, but rather to be used with the idea that some protection is better than none.

Many variations of the staccato method are possible, the essence of all being that one is secured to something for short sections of difficulty. One can, for example, use aid slings in place of rope. Used this way, the etriers extend from the climber as sort of tentacles, at least one and perferably two always grasping some point of security above before releasing those below.

FULL PITCH METHOD: This is best for aid climbing, and for free pitches where difficulties are sustained. Basically, it is a matter of fixing one end of the rope, attaching ascenders to it, and, with these ascenders attached to one's waist, moving them toward the other end of the rope as one climbs, clipping into points of protection along the way. After leading a pitch, slide down a second rope carried for that purpose and re-climb the pitch, removing the gear on the way. A haul sack can be brought up with the rappel line after cleaning the pitch.

One can, of course, use prusiks instead of ascenders or a combination of the two. But whatever one is using, it is wise to attach the rope to oneself by means of a figure-8 loop, at a distance of not more than 40 feet from the

Robbins in Buttermilk Country, Bishop, California
photo by Janet Roper

ascenders to act as a back-up if the prusiks or ascenders fail. If the nailing is thin the rope should be attached to the climber nearer the ascenders.

THE BARNETT SYSTEM: Steve Barnett developed a technique of self-belaying which appears to be superior to the traditional one outlined above. Bruce Carson, who used the system on the first solo ascent of the Integral on El Capitan, and on other serious routes, explained this method in an article published in *Summit,* April 1973. The great advantage of the Barnett System is it allows the rope to feed out while one is climbing.

HOW THE SYSTEM WORKS: The anchored rope runs through a pulley attached to the climber's chest loop, and then down through a "Penberthy style ascender knot."* This knot is part of a loop of rope which passes through the swami belt or other harness to be tied with a ring bend or grapevine knot. As the climber moves upward, the knot is raised by the rope and compressed against the pulley, allowing the rope to slide through the knot. If a fall occurs, the pulley is no longer held down by the pull on the rope, and no compression occurs on the knot, allowing it to do its job of gripping the rope and stopping the fall.

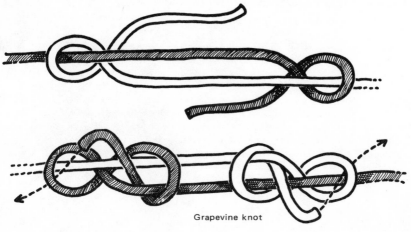

Grapevine knot

The only apparent disadvantage in this system is, as Carson says, "the amount of slack in the ascender knot is critical. Too little slack results in excessive friction through the system. More serious is too much slack. The knot may not catch in a fall. This can also happen if the sling rope is too rigid, if a prusik knot is used instead of an ascender knot, or if not enough turns of the sling rope are used around the climbing rope. The adjustment of the knot is mostly a matter of experience but a few points are clear. If a five-foot section of sling rope is used, about eight or nine turns around the climbing rope are necessary. If the sling rope doesn't wrap closely and smoothly around the climbing rope, it is probably too loose. A quick test is available to make sure the knot will hold; one merely pulls upward on the climbing rope to simulate a fall, and makes sure that the ascender knot grabs the climbing rope."

The ascender knot is tied by wrapping "a pliable sling rope around the climbing rope five to ten times, and joining the ends together such that the swami is included in the circle." The sling rope should be "the most pliable and limp nylon available, in 8, 9, or 10 mm diameter. It is critical that the

*All quotes in this chapter from: B. Carson, "A New Solo Climbing System," *Summit,* April 1973.

rope be unprocessed (i.e., not heat-treated), such as is available at many marine supply stores." Processed rope will be too stiff for this use.

The Barnett System appears especially useful for self-belayed free climbing, as it leaves the hands free to grab rock. In difficult free climbing, the figure-8 tie-in for the back-up should be as close to the ascender knot as possible, but far enough away to allow one to reach a ledge where the hands can be freed to adjust the back-up knot. If the climbing is sustained, or if one is uncertain where one can stop, it might be useful to tie several loose figure-8's at spaced intervals along the rope and attach all of these to one's swami. These back-ups can be quickly untied one after another as the climber reaches them and the successive back-up knots would be already in place. The unclipping and untieing can be easily done using only a single hand with the help of one's teeth.

There are as many variations on the above themes as you can imagine, but any methods adopted should be subjected to thorough experimentation in safe conditions.

FREE SOLO: One attraction of unroped soloing is that it enables one to climb faster. This is especially true when experts are on rock that is only moderately difficult. An expert can, without a rope, safely climb such rock quickly and without hesitation. Or, he may carry a rope and use it only on short sections of more difficult climbing. In the mountains, when speed means safety, such soloing has its practical advantages. In pure rockclimbing, however, free soloing is attractive not for its safety but for the joy of moving competently and unfettered with only the belay of one's mind and body working smoothly to produce an art — to be high above the ground yet be in complete control, but know that such control comes only from mastery of the rock and of oneself.

COMPETITION: Unroped soloing by an expert in the proper state of mind can be a joyful experience, and on difficult routes it is an accomplishment. But accomplishments lead to praise, praise to envy, envy to competition, competition, in a game like this, to climbing beyond one's limits — that morbid note. Sometimes waves of soloing competition will pass over climbing centers, as the stars try to outdo each other in pushing the fine line. These waves pass, as by and by the soloists feel the old reaper looking over their shoulders, and they look at the rocks below and realize that only a moment's lack of concentration, a split second's faltering in will or attention, and they will be off the rock with the ground coming up very fast, and all because competition led them to try what they wouldn't have attempted for pure joy of climbing.

TECHNIQUE: If one must solo unroped, the technique is much the same as used by the leader embarking on a poorly protected pitch. The difference is that there is even less room for error. This is the most critical aspect of free soloing — that the smallest mistake or misjudgement can be fatal. For this reason the free solo game is the most severe of rockclimbing disciplines.

Cenotaph Corner, Llanberis Pass, North Wales

Luck isn't involved, or shouldn't be. One must never take a chance soloing; never try something unless one *knows* one can do it. The expert rockclimber does not leave his fate in the hands of chance, because he realizes there is no merit in succeeding through luck, and because he knows luck inevitably runs out.

One of the most persistent hazards of free soloing is climbing into a position from which retreat is impossible. This is an especially tricky problem in steep face climbing, where it is usually easier to climb up than down. It is imperative for the soloist, as for the roped leader climbing without good protection, to be very alert to avoid getting stuck. He must not make moves he cannot reverse. To avoid making that mistake he might take hours working out a series of moves, or leave them undone and prudently retreat.

In short, though he may be moved by romantic notions of the freedom of soloing, the most unromantic common sense must govern the soloist's actions on rock.

But even if he attempts only what he *knows* he can do, there is still a way to get the chop. The terrible thing about free soloing difficult routes that are within one"s capacity, is the chance that faced with ultimate danger and need for ultimate self-control, one's nerve might fail and cause an error. That's the irony of it — that fear could short-circuit skill, that one would die as a direct result of being afraid to die.

So before you take leave of your friends, consider well the seriousness and and possible consequences of going alone.

Values

We have dealt with the pragmatic aspects of climbing, with climbing as science. There remains to be said something about the principles which guide the use of equipment and technique. Central to this discussion is the concept of climbing as art.

NEW ROUTES ARE CREATIONS

Climbing as science can take us only so far. When we bring the practical and definable elements together, and light them with a bit of spiritual fire, we may produce something new and unique, such as a first ascent. A first ascent involves artistic creation in several ways. One of these is common to all climbing, whether first ascents or not. This is the control, cunning, and craft used by the leader in getting up — that is, his artful use of body, of holds, of means of resting and saving his strength, and his choice of runners and skill in placing them and making them stay. This area of the leader's self-expression is like a dance which he choreographs as he goes. It is uniquely his own, and ephemeral — it doesn't last, but he can create another like every time he touches rock. And so can all climbers, whether leaders or followers, first ascenders or not.

THE LINE

A second aspect of the first ascent as creation is the line the leader selects. In some cases there will be small scope for creativity here, as when the route simply follows a chimney for 300 feet. But at other times working out a line which wends a serpentine way up an obscure face, or through apparently impassable overhangs may be an act of brilliant creativity which over shadows the quality of the climbing on the route.

DEFINING THE GAME

A third aspect of creativity in first ascents is the aids the leader rejects. In these days when any rock can be climbed by the use of irresistible technology, the limits set by the leader on what he uses is of critical importance in constructing a route, and gives great scope for personal expression. Thus, a party might freely use all the chocks they wish, but avoid pitons. They might decide to take or not take a hammer, or a bolt kit. Or, as has been done recently, they might take bolts and chocks but no pitons, and place a bolt as a permanent anchor any time chocks won't suffice.

With the combination of choices including the way one climbs, the exact route one chooses, and the selection of limits set on aids, a party making a first ascent has infinite opportunities for artistic creation.

I wish to place in the reader's mind a picture of a route as not just a line, but rather a composite of line and style forming a whole which we call a creation. Viewing climbing in this way leads to an easier understanding of the first ascent principle proposed in *Basic Rockcraft,* which called for a hands-off policy toward routes even if the style in which they were done makes us gag. That principle presupposes an attitude which recognizes that a first ascent is a creation in the same sense as is a painting or a song. Though we may find a painting execrable, we respect it as a creative effort, and do not, if civilized, slash it with a knife, or even add a dab of a paint. We do not chop or place bolts on a route because of our respect for other's creations, and because of our consideration for the feelings of all the climbers in the future who might want to repeat the route as it was originally done. So we honor the route and the creative effort by leaving it as nearly intact as possible. If this principle is generally adhered to, we can have large numbers of climbers without degrading routes.

OUTRAGES

There is, however, an area not discussed in *Basic Rockcraft,* which concerns first ascents done in a style which lies significantly outside the *mores* of a climbing center. Creations on rock are different from creations on canvas in that the medium is limited and belongs to everyone. And although anyone has a "right" to make a first ascent by placing bolts up blank walls, the same right must be granted in terms of removing the bolts. It is not too much to expect a due regard for the values generally held in a climbing center. Thus for an American to visit Britain and put a new route on Dinas Cromlech by placing bolts would be boorish. It would reveal a gross insensitivity toward the values of the locals whose sense of style kept them from

climbing the route in such a manner. One would not be surprised if they exercised their right of removing the offending bolts, much as they did the pitons of the Munich Climb in the Thirties. Similarly, if someone put up a bolt route next to Horseman in the Shawangunks, he would be ill-advised to expect his ascent to be honored, or even to find its way into the guidebook. A local consensus would probably decree that it go. Another example is a route in Tuolumne Meadows which was established by pre-placing bolts on rappel. That route is gone, and no one is weeping. We should not expect that our first ascent principle should apply in all cases. There are exceptions.

ETHICS

Along these lines is a question of ethics not previously discussed, and this concerns competition for first ascents. In the scramble for new routes, there are times when those to whom success means more than style will resort to top-roping, pre-placing protection, or even the unforgivable chipping of holds. Such conduct is unethical if it leads to someone copping a first ascent by resorting to methods considered by the competition to be unsporting. There are precedents for top-roping and preplacing protection, but they are shaky ones. The argument is that the routes would not be done but for the employment of such methods. If true, perhaps they should be left undone. Why not a few monuments to Virginity? But more likely the claim is not true, as the history of the impossibles that have continually proven possible indicates. Perhaps the creation of a few particularly fine routes justifies preplacing of runners, but restraint is in order, for such precedents open the door to great abuse.

STYLE

In deciding the style in which one will do a new route, it is not amiss to consider the prevailing style of an area. Thus in Tuolumne Meadows one would expect to carry a bolt kit on a first ascent, but preplacing of bolts is held contemptible. On the other hand, at Lover's Leap, bolts themselves are *foreign*. They have been used only on one incomplete route there. Perhaps the Leap would be a good area to have a no-bolt ethic? The style should suit the area. What is good style here may be poor show there.

CREATIVE CLIMBING

The opportunities for creative climbing are not limited to first ascent parties. Everyone can do it. Climbers doing established routes have first of all their own creativity in getting themselves up. How others did a route in no way delimits the approach for subsequent parties. The fact that a crack is normally jammed, to take an easy example, doesn't argue for others not lie-backing it. And the number of possible variations of ways to get up a given section of rock is so great that one can be continuously creative here. The same is true regarding protection. One can be as inventive as the imagination will allow in getting runners on a pitch.

Another area of creativity on established routes lies in upward variations of the game, in doing the route in a more difficult style than the accepted mode. This aspect of creative climbing finds expression in doing aid routes free, in doing aid routes with nuts, in hammerless ascents, in not using "allowed" pitons or bolts, in soloing, and in many other ways. Usually the accepted mode of doing a climb is at least as high in terms of style as the first ascent. This is because, though the first ascenders may have been expert climbers, they were operating at a disadvantage in terms of knowledge and psychology. There are occasions, however, when the standard of the first ascent is not maintained. An example is Cenotaph Corner. That great Llanberian route is normally done using as many chock runners as one can place, but the first ascent involved only natural runners (plus the fixed pegs). One more nearly approaches what Joe Brown really created on the first ascent by limiting oneself to the same general type of protection (i.e., slings on horns, around chockstones, and threaded through holes).

CLIMBING FOR PLEASURE

But although a climber might set as a personal goal the ascent of a route in as good or better style than the first ascent party, it does not follow that others should feel constrained to follow that example. It is a bit much, for example, to expect a climber having an off-day to go down because he can't manage a short bit free, unless he is making a specific point of an all-free or no-go game. And it is a bit much to expect anyone to climb for any reason other than his own pleasure. If someone wants to use aid on the normal route of the Higher Spire, that surely is their business and no one else's. Let everyone climb as they please, as long as they don't interfere with the right of others to do the same.

FIXING THE CONCEPT

The concept of climbs as not just lines, but as creations combining line and style, can lead to an incredibly rich variety of climbing games. Those making first ascents will be conscious of everything they are doing because it will all be part of their creation. They will not just be getting from bottom to top, but will in effect be writing a score. That piton they are thinking of placing will not be trivial, but will be of enormous importance. Like a single word in a poem, it can effect the entire composition.

If we wish to encourage this concept, two things will help. Those who do a new route can, besides describing it, indicate what game they were playing. If they were, for example, trying to limit the pitons used, then this was part of the game, and an indication of where the pitons are placed (or fixed) would be helpful to subsequent parties wishing to repeat the creation of the originators. The other avenue to fixing the concept is for guidebooks to give the style of the first ascent, as specifically as possible, as well as describe where the route goes and telling how hard it is. Then parties wishing to re-create as nearly as possible the first ascent, or wishing to play a harder game, will have the information which will enable them to do so.

TECHNOLOGY AND WHAT TO DO WITH IT

Technology in climbing is both a blessing and a curse; it expands the limits of the possible but robs us of adventure. Since it is technology which makes anything in rockclimbing possible, it is technology which we must selectively reject in order to have limits to the possible, for without limits there is no game. Since every year there are new technological innovations, we must be constantly making decisions about whether to use a new device and in what circumstances. There are two main areas of concern here, one is first ascents and the other is repeats. Regarding first ascents, technology has led, in Messner's phrase, to the murder of the impossible. With quickie methods of bolting, anyone with the patience can in 20 days place a route straight up any five-foot wide section of rock on El Capitan. We are, however, not primarily concerned with the problems of technological omnipotence as relates to first ascents. After all, first ascenders have great scope, as long as they stay this side of outrages. And a technological innovation such as an extension rod for placing runners may eliminate need for bolts on a new route.

But what we do with new equipment on established routes is different. If our aim is to experience as nearly as possible the creation of the originators, to face the problems they faced with the same limited means, then the use of an extension rod on a route done without it is not the same thing. In fact, the difference of an extra two feet of reach might be critical, it might possibly eliminate the point of the climb as seen through the eyes of the first ascenders. Similarly with large chocks in wide cracks first climbed without them. And so it goes in various degrees with knee-pads, tape for hands, chalk, topos, rivets, and, eventually, suction cups. *If* one is concerned with not letting technology get between oneself and the creation put up by the pioneers of a route, there is a simple solution: limit our arsenal to match theirs. This brings us back to respecting what the creation is, and climbing within its limits, knowing that we may make it easier for ourselves if we wish, but being conscious that we are doing so.

Of course, one can easily slip into absurdity. I'm not advocating using nailed boots on the classic rock climbs of the Alps, or tennis shoes instead of rock shoes, or steel carabiners instead of aluminum, or machine nuts instead of chocks designed for climbing, even out of respect for the way a first ascent was done. We accept some technical innovations as standard, while rejecting others. One will have a personal style, and way of approaching climbing games. What will be not pure enough for one person will be acceptable for another. It's a question of personal choice, and the individual need answer to no one but himself for his decisions. But it is good to understand the issues, and to make one's choices consciously. The more one understands the questions involved and the options, the more will one be able, in one's own climbing, to be creative.

The chapter which follows is a story of a climb. It is included in the hope of giving life to some of the dry, instructional prose which has gone before, of conveying some of the reality of the climbing experience, of showing some of the things which give rockclimbing its richness, of indicating why I love it.

FANTASIA

Kent hailed from England. He knew the Grit, and Harrison's. He had savored the Rock of the Ben, and been on the Isle of Lundy. He knew North Wales, had done a book on the Black Crag. Sea Cliffs? Gogarth his favorite, but never disdained to grab rock at Swanage or Cornwall. His fingers had stroked the limestone of Avon and the Pennines. And he had more than a nodding acquaintance with the Jewels of the Lake District. He was, in fact, an authority on British climbing, with a book soon coming to prove it.

Kent had come to sample the wonders of the Valley, to taste the climbing, the rocks, the social scene. I lured him from the hot bed of the climbing game, the arena of competition, of mangled hands and knees, exultation and despair, arrogance and sycophancy, where the sun shines So Hot. A tight, noisy place. Actually, most of that rather suited Kent, but he was tempted by my tales of a northern crag, of routes with sufficient character, and beauty, and variety, to please his connoisseur's palate. And maybe a first ascent! He decided to come. There might be a chance for good copy. Perhaps I would fall.

"What a crag," whooped Kent, as we treaded along the old jeep trail beneath the cliff. "It looks nearly good." Nearly good was Kent's highest praise.

"It's as high as Cloggy," I observed, "though it's not yet got as many routes. Perhaps we'll add one today."

I pointed out the lines. "Corrugation Corner is just there, that dihedral, a super route — steep, makes you think, but not extreme. And just to its left — Travelers — takes that lower pillar, and then up the crack in the face, around to the right, and then, very exciting, back around, and up the edge, straight up. It's called Travelers because of that pink rock there. A subtle name, a period piece of the fifties. And that deep chimney is Eeyore's — had a good day there with Dorworthy last winter, one of the most demanding days I've had. But that seems to happen whenever I climb with Dorworthy." I pointed out Hourglass, Eagle Buttress, Letter Box, and nightmarish Incubus, a savage route. "And there's the Line," I said, pointing to a crack tracing a plumb line up the vertical 300 foot face of the East Wall. "The first pitch is as good as Cenotaph Corner." I knew Kent would appreciate this comparison.

[85]

But our objective was further on, nearly to the end of the cliff. "That's Haystack on the left, and over there is Scimitar, put up by Coving, Tun, and Urb. Our line will go up between them."

"Will it?" said Kent.

"Well, it's meant to. I was supposed to do this route with Rope, but he's off flying. He's always off flying. He's crazy, you know. We're all crazy."

Our proposed route lay up a rounded buttress nearly devoid of vertical cracks. We would have to pick our way up the horizontal striations peculiar to this rock, weaving back and forth to avoid the blank areas. It looked chancy whether it would go. "You might waste your only day here," I said, "but we can have some good fun trying."

"Great, let's go," beamed Kent.

We left the path and in the blue light of mountain shade moved through tough scrub oak, and over rickety, rectangular blocks of talus, quickly reaching the rock.

An arch curved up rightwards. I followed it, though I could just as easily have climbed straight up, for the rock is striped with horizontal bands sandwiched between layers of less resistent rock, and forming ledges of varying dimensions, sometimes quite small and brittle. One has, therefore, a sort of natural ladder which sometimes makes the climbing quite easy. But when the angle is steep, and it generally is here, these ledges, while offering a way up, also hold out the danger of luring one into a trap, for runners are sometimes scarce, and it is hard to climb down. It is an area where technical competence combined with "attack", if freed from the chain of prudence, can easily lead to becoming airborne.

At the top of the arch I was 40 feet up without a runner. It was easy. Then it got hard fast. The rock suddenly steepened to overhanging. It was too steep to go straight up, but 15 feet left, above a singular patch of orange lichen the holds appeared to be better. It was strenuous looking. And scary. I took half an hour arranging my runners. Why? I was nearly scared. At the beginning of the traverse there was a small alcove with several cracks. I slotted two chocks and supported them with two pitons slipped gently into fissures from which, I reasoned, the direction of pull could not pluck them. I climbed up, struggling, and got a nut into a higher horizontal crack. Came down, panting and trembling with the effort. After a rest, I started the traverse. It was all on the arms, and when I was halfway there I saw in a flash two things: the overhang at the end of the traverse might not go, and if it didn't, I wouldn't have the strength to climb back, and a 30 foot swinging fall would result. So I geared up and hung on with weakening limbs and fought to secure another chock in the horizontal crack, near the end of the traverse. I struggled and grunted, and gasped, shifting first to one arm then to the other, desperately conserving what little strength I had, while trying to keep cool in the head, to think clearly about getting that chock slotted. Not very elegant, not very cool. Just a thrashing human sorting out his weaknesses and strengths above the rockwork orange.

Finally I got a good big nut secured and, attempting the hand traverse equivalent of stepping smartly, worked my way on weakening arms back

to the safety of the alcove. I braced a knee, dropped my arms, and panted.

Kent was enjoying it. "Hey Shann, were you freaked, man, were you freaked?" This came out with great glee and a twist of the word "freaked"; along with a physical seizure which hunched his shoulders, caused his head to shoot forward on a stiff neck, and his eyes to bulge. Kent loved Americanisms. He seemed to have a special fondness for the harsh, grating ones. One of his favorites was "trash", which he could repeat intermittently for hours on end. Adding "can" gave him even more pleasure. Whenever I offered him the rope, or carabiners, or water, or candy, he'd say "No thanks, throw it in the TRASH CAN." And then whisk it from my hands. "Yeah, Shann, you sure looked freaked; were you freaked?"

"Well, Kent," I replied, trying to restrain my thirst for oxygen, "you've got that American slang almost nearly right." This interchange so broke the tension that I burst out in hysterical laughter. Kent stared at me blankly, startled. He was dumbfounded by what tickled my funny bone. A rare occurrence, for Kent isn't often at a loss for words.

Soon the time had come for the big effort. I launched out, scared, but with confidence in the runners. I so wanted it to go, but I was so afraid it wouldn't. What if the holds just weren't there? There were no straight-forward pull-ups, as I had hoped. I didn't have time to work it all out, so I just went, and in several complicated, strenuous moves, was up. "Phew, heavy duty!" I shouted, borrowing a phrase from my friend Mac Not Davis. "It's just as good as it looks, a struggle, but it's all there."

"Will it go above the overhang" cried the belayer, looking up. I feebly answered "yes", and slowly crept on up. "We're not out of the woods yet, old boy." And so we weren't. But it was easy for a while. The striae were usable, though one wanted to keep on one's toes to avoid putting weight on the snapable edges.

I climbed 30 feet above the overhang, sans difficulty, sans runners. Then I was stopped by a smooth wall spotted with three grey knobs, like a triple-breasted woman. Things were getting woodier and woodier. A classic problem. Below the blank section was a long, narrow ledge, above it, jugs and safety. But it would take some doing to get from one to the other. Perhaps an all-out effort? Not up here. I was discouraged, but began, without much hope of success, to work it out.

The knob on the left was the highest, and it had a lip which might prevent a runner from slipping off, if the knob itself didn't break. Something about it suggested an inner corruption. Still, for want of anything better I laid on a sling of half-inch webbing. It was a "manky" runner. (As Kent digs Americanisms, so I am fascinated by Anglicisms. "Manky" has just the tone of disdain I felt, and just that implication of sinister unreliability that characterized my "protection.") I had to climb as if free solo, knowing at least, that if I did make a mistake, there was a chance I wouldn't go all the way.

The knob on the right (more of a rounded nubbin, really) was too far away to use. There were a couple of discolorations low on the face. These

Robbins leading an aid problem, Castle Rock, Boulder, Colo.

proved to be tiny bulges, which, though one couldn't stand on them, could nevertheless be used as toe holds and would take some of the weight off the fingers, the tips of which were dug into the lip on top of the left grey knob. I tested the holds, moving up, and carefully back down. Then up again and back down. It was going to be hard, which is to say getting up would require a major effort of creative climbing. I would have to combine a solution to the problem with self-control in working it out and in carrying it through. In short, I was going to have to do a little internal suffering. I didn't relish the prospect, but I did so want to get up.

I moved up again, feet higher, and stretched to feel with my left hand along the edge of a horizontal crack just at the end of my reach. Fingers moved along the edge, feeling, searching for that little ridge, or pocket which would make all the difference. Nothing. I carefully crept back down. After resting, I tried again. And again. There was an edge there, but not enough. Another approach. I moved up with my toes on the grey marks, my fingers biting intensely into the grey knob. Putting my left foot on the highest purchase I would find, I swung my right foot up to the center grey knob, placing the toe just so, and then pulled up with my fingers until my right foot was taking some weight. With the fingers of my left hand gripping the hold like life, I reached with my right hand for the horizontal crack. Ah! The edge was better over here. Distinctly better. It might yet go. And carefully, so carefully, climbed back down, to regain my strength. And consider. Then another try, same result. And again, and again. Each time I went up it was easier. My body was learning the movements. But still I couldn't do it. Each time I reached the apex, and felt the edge with the fingers of my right hand, I dared not let go my left hand, for I would be forced to do a one-arm pull-up onto my right foot. My fingers might slip or my strength might go. It was too chancy. And each time I failed I had to use the greatest precision in climbing down. I couldn't afford the luxury of a moment's carelessness.

There had to be a way. And then I saw it: The problem was that if I attempted to stand up with my foot on the center grey knob, my arm would be bending. It would take strength to pull up, and worse, as I got higher, there would be an outward pull on my fingers, and they might slip. If I could keep my arm straight . . . I was breathing hard in anticipation of the effort. Soon I was ready. It had to go. I sank my fingers into the grey knob. My toes moved to the smudges below: left foot, right, left, then the right leg arching up and the foot carefully set on the now familiar center knob. I pulled forward toward that foot, and up, reaching to my limit, fingers on the edge. I had it. Then . . . easy . . . I pivoted a bit, arching my back, getting more weight on the right foot, but keeping my right arm, its fingers gripping the high edge, extended. With a quick movement I took the fingers of my left hand from their grip and — this was the worst moment — turned my hand around and pressed the heel of it down on the sloping hold. I could then push *on my left hand, gaining six critical inches, and could move my other hand up and right to, as I had guessed, a more secure edge. My total being was focused on that right hand, and it pulled me up, up, until I could remove my left hand and replace it with my left foot. Phew, heavy duty! I was trembling with excitement and fear. What if it was harder up here than I anticipated? What if I couldn't get any runners? But not to worry. I searched around, found some good holds, and pulled up, moving with relief to a belay spot amid cracks, flakes, and small ledges. I fixed a couple of nuts, dropped a piton behind a flake, and looped a runner over a spike. "Come on up, Kent. It's a piece of cake."*

My friend armed across the traverse, and was almost armed out, as he pulled past the layered overhang. "Say, that tightens the forearms, doesn't it, Shann ol' boy? No place to hesitate!" He soon reached the grey knobs. He had trouble there, being unfamiliar with those peculiar turnsy, twisty, pushy techniques which one must master in the Valley. He tried, and reached, and fussed, and then got angry, and went for it, determined, and almost slipped, got his feet on the knobs, stood up, smiling, happy, and forgetting nearly good, exclaimed, "Hey, this climb is fantastic!"

ꝏ ꝏ ꝏ

"Good climbing and good company
often go together: each is essential to
the enjoyment of the other."

Tom Patey

Royal on Pacifico Rocks, age 16.
Photo by Bill Derr

Our boy, Royal, the author:

photo by Jim Stuart

Sheridan Andreas Mulholland Anderson, more familiarly known as "Sherry" though he prefers Rosé, is a completely undefinable character. A sign painter (billboard type), he is inclined to spend more of his time wandering about our Western mountain climbing haunts. His fey sense of humor contrasts strangely with his great accuracy of detail.

His drawings have appeared in SUMMIT, ASCENT, VULGARIAN DIGEST and other mountaineering journals, as well as in Royal's BASIC ROCKCRAFT.

Index

aid, 34
aid, leading, 35
anchors, 27
Armitage, John, 15

Barnett, Steve, 74, 75
bashies, 39
BASIC ROCKCRAFT, 7, 23, 35,
   47, 69, 79
belays, 27
belays, hanging, 55
big walls, 55ff
big walls, technique, 55
big walls, Yosemite method, 55
bivouacs, 58
bivouacs, hanging, 58
bongs, 26
bosses, 11

camming, 30
Carson, Bruce, 74
chickenheads, 11
chockcraft, 7ff, 70
chocks, removing, 29
chocks, reuse, 29
chocks, sling, 14
chocks, wired, 14
chockstones, 10
chockstones, artifical, 14
chockstones, natural, 10
Chouinard, Yvon, 7, 41
clean climbing, 7
cleaning, 45
coding, color, 17
competition, 77
copperheads, 22, 38, 39
cracks, horizontal, 22ff
creative climbing, 81

dangers, 63
descenders, 62
descender, figure 8, 62

devices, 53
El Capitan, 41, 74
ethics, 79
etriers, 35, 41
failure, equipment, 64
failure, judgment, 65
falls, 21
Fifi hooks, 42
first aid, 60
flakes, 11
flakes, loose, 28
food, 60
Forrest, Bill, 39
friction, 43
Frost, Tom, 15

gadgets, 61
gear, 60
hardnailing, 37
harnesses, 61
hauling, 57
hauling bags, 60
hazards, mountaineering, 63
helmet, safety, 61
hexcentrics, 19
horns, 11

jambed carabiners, 27
jambed knots, 27
Jumars, 45ff
Jumar removing, 47
Jumar safety, 52
Jumar seconding, 47

knots, 17

leader responsibility, 70
leading, 30ff, 66
lightning, 63
Logan hook, 41
Logan, Jim, 41
Lowe, Craig, 38

moss, 17
moving up, 41
nuts - see "artifical chockstones"

opposite-pressure, 23ff
outrages, 79
overhangs, 42, 49

pendulums, 49
pitons, nested, 35
piton tieoff, 35
placements, 35
practice, 43
practicing systems, 30
protection, 69

Robinson, Doug, 7
rope drag, 21, 70
rope-throwing, 41
route finding, 66
route selection, 67
runners, 13
runners, natural, 10
RURPS, 39

safety, 63
self control, 70
self pulley, 43
sharp diagonals, 49

skyhooks, 41
slings, 10, 13, 47
smashies, 39
soloing, Barnett system, 73
solo climbing, 70
soloing, free, 77
soloing, full pitch, 73
soloing, roped, 73
soloing, staccato, 73
Stannard, John, 7, 15, 22
Sticht plate, 62, 63
style, 81
SUMMIT Magazine, 7, 23, 38,
   74, 75

Tahquitz, 65
technology, 82
traverses, tension, 49, 51, 70
The Line, 78
trees and bushes, 11
tunnels and arches, 11

UIAA, 19

water, 60
webbing, 15

Yosemite, 35

La Siesta Press